DO OUR BELIEFS AFFECT THE WAY WE SOUND?
THE PHENOMENON OF SECOND LANGUAGE PRONUNCIATION

Editora Appris Ltda.
1.ª Edição - Copyright© 2024 da autora
Direitos de Edição Reservados à Editora Appris Ltda.

Nenhuma parte desta obra poderá ser utilizada indevidamente, sem estar de acordo com a Lei nº 9.610/98. Se incorreções forem encontradas, serão de exclusiva responsabilidade de seus organizadores. Foi realizado o Depósito Legal na Fundação Biblioteca Nacional, de acordo com as Leis nos 10.994, de 14/12/2004, e 12.192, de 14/01/2010.

Catalogação na Fonte
Elaborado por: Josefina A. S. Guedes
Bibliotecária CRB 9/870

B732d
2024
	Borges, Laís de Oliveira
	   Do our beliefs affect the way we sound? The phenomenon of second language pronunciation / Laís de Oliveira Borges – 1. ed. – Curitiba: Appris, 2024.
	   120 p. ; 21 cm. – (Linguagem e literatura).
	
	   Inclui referência.
	   ISBN 978-65-250-5888-7
	
	   1. Língua inglesa – Estudo e ensino. 2. Língua inglesa – Pronúncia. 3. Língua inglesa – Fonemática. I. Título. II. Série.
	
	                                                                CDD – 428.24

Livro de acordo com a normalização técnica da APA

Appris *editora*

Editora e Livraria Appris Ltda.
Av. Manoel Ribas, 2265 – Mercês
Curitiba/PR – CEP: 80810-002
Tel. (41) 3156 - 4731
www.editoraappris.com.br

Printed in Brazil
Impresso no Brasil

Laís de Oliveira Borges

DO OUR BELIEFS AFFECT THE WAY WE SOUND?
THE PHENOMENON OF SECOND LANGUAGE PRONUNCIATION

FICHA TÉCNICA

EDITORIAL	Augusto Coelho
	Sara C. de Andrade Coelho
COMITÊ EDITORIAL	Marli Caetano
	Andréa Barbosa Gouveia - UFPR
	Edmeire C. Pereira - UFPR
	Iraneide da Silva - UFC
	Jacques de Lima Ferreira - UP
SUPERVISOR DA PRODUÇÃO	Renata Cristina Lopes Miccelli
ASSESSORIA EDITORIAL	Sabrina Costa
REVISÃO	Stephanie Ferreira Lima
PRODUÇÃO EDITORIAL	Sabrina Costa
DIAGRAMAÇÃO	Jhonny Alves dos Reis
CAPA	Mateus de Andrade Porfírio
REVISÃO DE PROVA	Raquel Fuchs

COMITÊ CIENTÍFICO DA COLEÇÃO LINGUAGEM E LITERATURA

DIREÇÃO CIENTÍFICA Erineu Foerste (UFES)

CONSULTORES

- Alessandra Paola Caramori (UFBA)
- Alice Maria Ferreira de Araújo (UnB)
- Célia Maria Barbosa da Silva (UnP)
- Cleo A. Altenhofen (UFRGS)
- Darcília Marindir Pinto Simões (UERJ)
- Edenize Ponzo Peres (UFES)
- Eliana Meneses de Melo (UBC/UMC)
- Gerda Margit Schütz-Foerste (UFES)
- Guiomar Fanganiello Calçada (USP)
- Ieda Maria Alves (USP)
- Ismael Tressmann (Povo Tradicional Pomerano)
- Joachim Born (Universidade de Giessen/Alemanha)
- Leda Cecília Szabo (Univ. Metodista)
- Letícia Queiroz de Carvalho (IFES)
- Lidia Almeida Barros (UNESP-Rio Preto)
- Maria Margarida de Andrade (UMACK)
- Maria Luisa Ortiz Alvares (UnB)
- Maria do Socorro Silva de Aragão (UFPB)
- Maria de Fátima Mesquita Batista (UFPB)
- Maurizio Babini (UNESP-Rio Preto)
- Mônica Maria Guimarães Savedra (UFF)
- Nelly Carvalho (UFPE)
- Rainer Enrique Hamel (Universidad do México)

In memory of José Borges de Moura.

ACKNOWLEDGMENTS

There are many I would like to thank and without whom this book may never have come to fruition: the TESOL team at the Institute of Education, University College London, especially Dr. Amos Paran and Dr. Andrea Révész; the participants who generously agreed to take part in the study; my parents, Dr. Cibele Brandão and Dr. Antônio de Moura Borges, who have done so much - I can only dream of following in your footsteps; Marcella, for inspiring me to publish this book; my extended family, especially Dr. Teresinha Campos and Dr. Paulo Borges; and my grandfather, José Borges de Moura, who left the fields of rural Brazil to study in the city where he eventually became a lawyer – I wish you were still here with us.

PREFACE

The prevalent phonologically oriented studies of second language acquisition focus on external factors – for example, age of learning onset or length of residence in an L2 environment. Such variables give teachers and learners little direction as to how learners can improve their pronunciation competence in the target language. One area which seems important in terms of internal factors is pronunciation beliefs, and awareness of which beliefs about second language acquisition appear detrimental to pronunciation attainment serves as a first step towards the development of classroom practices and materials aimed at reshaping these views. The present volume engages with two important areas - pronunciation and socio-psychological factors – and with the different research methods associated with these areas. It investigates the relationship between pronunciation accuracy and pronunciation beliefs of English as a second language (ESL) learners and is an important contribution to our understanding of the intersection between them.

To summarise, the study correlates the beliefs of Brazilian ESL learners with pronunciation scores, according to native speaker judgments. The questionnaire about pronunciation beliefs was constructed specially for this study, based on findings from previous studies, reported in a wide-ranging survey of the research literature. The questionnaire integrated interrelated socio-psychological variables such as learner attitudes, language anxiety, motivation, willingness to communicate, self-confidence beliefs, and language learning strategies. The questionnaire comprised seven scales: Emotional Beliefs, Self-Confidence Beliefs, Beliefs about Pronunciation Acquisition, Beliefs about Pronunciation Instruction, Functional Beliefs, Beliefs about Pronunciation Learning Strategies, and Cultural Beliefs. The instrument also included items referring to pronunciation self-ratings and respondents' factual information. Participants were asked to rate themselves against statements about pronunciation, along a 6-point Likert scale.

After completing the questionnaire, each participant (N = 30) participated in three tasks: a word reading task; a sentence reading task; and a free-response task. The speech samples were normalized and initial dysfluencies removed. Three judges listened to the pronunciation tasks and rated each participant on a scale of 1-9. Pearson-Product Moment correlation analyses were performed with subjects' mean ratings on the pronunciation tasks and their mean scores on questionnaire items. Bivariate correlations were computed for learners' pronunciation self-ratings and judges' assessments. To determine possible confounding factors, pronunciation ratings were also correlated with language background variables.

Two of the scales showed significant correlations with pronunciation accuracy as measured by the ratings of the three raters. Emotional beliefs showed a moderate negative correlation ($r=-.49$, $p<.01$), indicating that students who declared lower levels of pronunciation anxiety were likely to be more successful at the phonological component of the target language. Self-confidence beliefs showed a moderate positive correlation ($r=.42$, $p<.05$), demonstrating that students who were confident about their accent obtained higher scores on judges' ratings. Beliefs about pronunciation acquisition and instruction, functional beliefs, pronunciation learning goals, learning strategies, and cultural beliefs did not affect pronunciation outcomes. Of the language background factors, age of onset of learning was the only factor which exerted an effect on the outcome.

In sum, the results indicated that pronunciation accuracy is most significantly affected by emotional beliefs associated with the target language pronunciation, followed by self-confidence beliefs. In relation to language background variables, as expected, age of onset was found to be a predictor of outcome. The study concludes that negative beliefs associated with affective factors appear to be detrimental to L2 phonological attainment.

Crucially, the findings reported in this volume highlight the importance of reducing learners' anxiety regarding their pronunciation and of enhancing their self-confidence in this area of language learning, suggesting that reducing anxiety and raising self-confidence should become primary objectives in the pronunciation classroom. Language educators can achieve this by encouraging their students' involvement in classroom activities, creating a comfortable learning atmosphere, providing guidance, and fostering learners' self-directness and pro-activity. Findings from future research will prove to be particularly fruitful in helping us integrate practices which are conducive to pronunciation attainment into the second language classroom.

Amos Paran
Professor of TESOL
Co-Director, Centre for Applied Linguistics
IOE, UCL's Faculty of Education and Society
University College London, UK

LIST OF ABBREVIATIONS

ALM	–	Audio-Lingual Method
AO	–	Age of Onset
BALLI	–	Beliefs About Language Learning Inventory
CLT	–	Communicative Language Teaching
CPH	–	Critical Period Hypothesis
EFL	–	English as a Foreign Language
ELF	–	English as a Lingua Franca
ESL	–	English as a Second Language
ESOL	–	English to Speakers of Other Languages
FL	–	Foreign Language
FLCAS	–	Foreign Language Classroom Anxiety Scale
ID	–	Individual Differences
L1	–	First Language or First Languages
L2	–	Second Language, used as an umbrella term referring to both second and foreign languages, unless otherwise specified.
LA	–	Language Anxiety
LOR	–	Length of Residence
NNS	–	Non-native Speaker
NS	–	Native Speaker
PAI	–	Pronunciation Attitude Inventory
SLA	–	Second Language Acquisition
TELT	–	Training and Education of Language Teachers
TESOL	–	Teaching English to Speakers of Other Languages

CONTENTS

CHAPTER ONE
INTRODUCTION 17
  Why pronunciation? 17
  Predictors of phonological performance: the impact of socio-affective
  factors 18

CHAPTER TWO
SOCIO-PSYCHOLOGICAL FACTORS AND L2 PRONUNCIATION ACHIEVEMENT 21
  2.1 *Research on L2 pronunciation acquisition and instruction* 21
  2.2 *The socio-psychological dimension of L2 phonological attainment* 24
  2.3 *An overview of learner beliefs* 31
  2.4 *Learner beliefs about L2 pronunciation* 34
  2.5 *Studies of successful phonological attainment* 36
  2.6 *Conclusions* 38

CHAPTER THREE
PREDICTORS OF L2 PHONOLOGICAL PERFORMANCE - THE CASE OF BRAZILIAN ESL LEARNERS 41
  3.1 *Population and Sample* 41
  3.2 *Questionnaire Design* 42
  3.3 *Rating-judgment study* 43
    3.3.1 *Raters* 44
    3.3.2 *Scale* 45
    3.3.3 *Stimuli* 45
  3.4 *Procedures* 47

CHAPTER FOUR
EXAMINING THE IMPACT OF BELIEFS ABOUT PRONUNCIATION ON L2 PHONOLOGICAL PERFORMANCE 49

4.1 *Data Analysis* 49
4.2 *Pronunciation mean scores* 50
4.3 *Beliefs about pronunciation: significant construct correlations* 51
4.4 *Beliefs about pronunciation: significant item correlations* 54
4.5 *Beliefs about pronunciation: non-significant construct correlations* 57
4.6 *Self-assessment and language background variables* 63
4.7 *Summary of results* 65

CHAPTER FIVE
THE ROLE OF SOCIO-AFFECTIVE FACTORS ON L2 PRONUNCIATION ATTAINMENT 67
5.1 *Emotional beliefs* 67
5.2 *Self-confidence beliefs* 68
5.3 *The effects of affective variables on pronunciation attainment* 70
5.4 *Demographic factors: age of onset* 71

CHAPTER SIX
CONCLUSIONS 75
6.1 *Summary of research findings* 75
6.2 *Limitations of the study* 76
6.3 *Pedagogical and theoretical implications* 77

REFERENCES 79

APPENDICES 93

Chapter One

INTRODUCTION

This volume is based on my Master's dissertation (Institute of Education, University College London), which comprises an empirical study about the effects of pronunciation beliefs on the phonological attainment of Brazilian learners of L2 English. This study was selected to go forward to the British Council Dissertation Award Scheme by the Applied Linguistics, TESOL team at University College London, and was awarded a commendation for best contribution to English Language Teaching, British Council, 2014.

Why pronunciation?

An increasing body of research in the field of second language acquisition (SLA) indicates that unfamiliar accents hamper listening comprehension for both native and non-native listeners (e.g., Munro & Derwing 1995; Derwing & Munro, 1997; Major, Fitzmaurice, Bunta & Balasubramanian, 2002). These studies demonstrate that second language (L2)[1] accented speech has a direct impact on communication, which is for the most part the primary aim of foreign language learning. Since pronunciation plays a significant role in successful communication, its study should be an important aspect within interactively oriented teaching and learning contexts.

Yet, the study of L2 pronunciation has been neglected for many years within applied linguistics, while grammatical and vocabulary

---

[1] In the field of Sociolinguistics, the term 'additional language' has been increasingly adopted to refer to the acquisition of language whereby neither the geographical context nor the order in which the language is acquired by the speaker (L2, L3 etc.) is of particular relevance.
Following the SLA literature, the term 'second language' (L2) will be used in this book to refer to the acquisition and learning of a non-native language in any linguistic situation. No social or political distinction is intended here.

skills remain predominant areas of inquiry in the field (Derwing & Munro, 2005). Consequently, pronunciation is widely omitted from foreign language curricula and, when included, commonsense intuitive notions—rather than empirical evidence—often inform classroom practices and priorities (Breitkreutz, Derwing & Rossiter, 2001). In the last decades, however, there has been a heightened interest in pronunciation among SLA researchers which can be attested by the recent increase in publications within the field (e.g., Hua, 2023; Saito, 2023; Isaacs & Harding, 2017). Despite the rise in stature of pronunciation research, only recently have investigators turned to studies which contemplate the effects of individual differences on the learning of this skill.

Predictors of phonological performance: the impact of socio-affective factors

My motivation for researching learners' beliefs about pronunciation attainment stemmed from the need to address an ongoing issue within the area. The prevalent phonologically oriented studies of second language acquisition focus on external factors such as age of learning onset or cross-language influences in the perception and production of L2 phonology[2]. These variables give both instructors and learners little direction as to how learners may improve their pronunciation competence in the target language.

Understanding the extent to which learners' views about L2 pronunciation influence phonological achievement and which of these beliefs appear to contribute to higher levels of phonological attainment will assist language teachers in identifying reasons for their learners' success or failure in attaining higher levels of pronunciation ability. This knowledge can enable instructors to offer students the opportunity to modify their beliefs in a favorable direction.

---

[2] Following SLA research conventions, the term 'phonology' will be adopted throughout this book to encompass both phonetics and phonology. While the former refers to the system of discrete speech sounds in a language, the latter relates to the rules governing the relationships between sounds, e.g., elision, deletion, stress patterns etc.

Awareness of which beliefs about second language acquisition appear to be detrimental to pronunciation attainment can therefore assist in the construction of classroom practices and materials aimed at reshaping these views.

Research on learners' beliefs about L2 pronunciation is scant (e.g., Burri, 2023; Hua, 2023; Simon & Taveniers, 2011; Cenoz & Lecumberi, 1999; Sobkowiak, 2002). Furthermore, few studies to date have empirically investigated the ways in which beliefs about pronunciation affect learners' phonological performance in the target language. The present volume attempts to fill this gap in the literature.

The purpose of the study reported in this book is therefore to determine which beliefs about L2 pronunciation are associated with success in this skill among Brazilian learners of L2 English. The research also addresses the questions: (a) Do these successful learners share a particular set of beliefs about L2 pronunciation? (b) Are successful learners' beliefs about L2 pronunciation in accordance with research on L2 phonological attainment? (c) Is pronunciation accuracy confounded with other demographic variables?

To address these questions, the first stage of data collection involved the employment of a self-devised questionnaire. In the next stage, a rating-judgment study (e.g., Derwing & Munro, 2005; Major *et al.,* 2002; Derwing & Munro, 1997; Munro & Derwing, 1995) was conducted to determine participants' levels of phonological performance. At this stage of the research, three native-speaker judges rated the accents of 30 Brazilian ESL learners, and their blind responses determined subjects' levels of pronunciation competence. Statistical analyses then revealed correlations between subjects' pronunciation beliefs and their levels of phonological attainment.

The study reported in this volume hopes to contribute towards an accurate understanding of successful learners' perceptions about pronunciation acquisition, which can ultimately lead to the development of instructional strategies aimed at restructuring beliefs of poor language learners. This research is not only significant to the population it investigates, but also to a broader picture of L2 English learners since a deeper understanding of the socio-psychological aspects involved in L2 phonological attainment is fundamental for the development of appropriate pronunciation pedagogies.

The remaining of this book is organized in the following manner: **Chapter Two** provides the background for the main themes of the research. In the first part of the chapter, I will present a review of the literature on the acquisition and instruction of L2 pronunciation, and will then move on to focus more specifically on the area of socio-psychological aspects of phonological attainment. Next, a brief overview of learner beliefs about SLA is provided, followed by an examination of studies on learner beliefs about L2 pronunciation. Studies that have investigated predictors of pronunciation accuracy are then listed.

Chapter Three describes the methods employed in the study, its population and sample, the procedures involved in data collection, and the analysis of data. In **Chapter Four** I present a summary of statistical findings. **Chapter Five** provides a discussion of the results in light of previous research. Finally, **Chapter Six** concludes the study, and includes its limitations, pedagogical implications, as well as suggestions for future research.

Chapter Two

SOCIO-PSYCHOLOGICAL FACTORS AND L2 PRONUNCIATION ACHIEVEMENT

This chapter provides a brief overview of L2 pronunciation research and examines the ways in which socio-psychological aspects of L2 acquisition and learning inform L2 phonological attainment. Next, learner beliefs about SLA are discussed and the existent, though limited, literature on beliefs about L2 pronunciation is evaluated. Finally, research on predictors of success in phonological attainment is presented.

2.1 *Research on L2 pronunciation acquisition and instruction*

An increasing body of research in the field of second language acquisition (SLA) indicates that unfamiliar accents hamper listening comprehension for both native and nonnative listeners (see for example Munro & Derwing 1995; Derwing & Munro, 1997 and Major, Fitzmaurice, Bunta & Balasubramanian, 2002). These studies demonstrate that L2 accented speech has a direct impact on communication, which is for the most part the primary aim of foreign language learning. In fact, not only does pronunciation play a significant role on successful communication, but it also affects L2 users' personal and social lives (Setter & Jenkins, 2005). L2 accented speech is therefore a complex aspect of language that affects individuals both productively and receptively, as well as in social interaction (Derwing & Munro, 2005).

Seen in this light, the value of phonology instruction in second and foreign language learning becomes conspicuous, yet Isaacs (2009) reports that pronunciation has been neglected for many years within the field of applied linguistics. As we shall see, trends in SLA research and L2 instruction have often contributed to the marginalization of phonology from the TESL mainstream.

Pronunciation enjoyed a position of prominence in the Audio-Lingual Method (ALM) of second and foreign language learning, with its emphasis on traditional notions of L2 phonological acquisition (Otlowski, 1998). After the decline in popularity of the ALM in the 1960s and 1970s, L2 phonology research and instruction suffered a setback with the advent of Communicative Language Teaching (CLT) in the early 1980s (Hammond, 1995). The notion that pronunciation is an acquired skill which cannot be taught also became highly influential among L2 researchers and professionals in the 1970s and early 1980s. This assumption is attributed to Krashen, who claimed that the factors which affect the acquisition of L2 pronunciation cannot be altered by focused practice or the systematic teaching of rules (1982 in Jones, 1997).

The prominence of the *Critical Period Hypothesis* (CPH) in SLA research has also contributed to this view. Starting with the work of Lenneberg (1967), the CPH entails the notion that there is a neurological period, ending at the onset of puberty, beyond which mastery of a second language is no longer achievable. Lenneberg's hypothesis disseminated the popular belief that aiming for nativelike pronunciation is an unattainable goal for adult learners.

In recent decades, however, research in L2 phonology has attempted to demonstrate that "there seems to be no justification for denying learners linguistic information which may empower them to improve on their own" (Jones, 1997, p. 108). Indeed, a plethora of strategies for incorporating pronunciation instruction within a communicative framework have been proposed over the years (see for example Levis, 1999; Isaacs, 2009 and Trofimovich, 2013).

In spite of this growing interest in the component of phonology, pronunciation instruction is still not provided to students within ESL learning contexts. L2 practitioners, who generally have received very little, if any, formal teacher training in phonology instruction, tend to avoid pronunciation in language classrooms (Burgess & Spencer, 2000; Breitkreutz, Derwing & Rossiter, 2001). Meanwhile, when pronunciation is included in the language curriculum, rather than being grounded in solid research, classroom practices and priorities are largely determined by commonsense intuitive notions (Derwing & Munro, 2005). To address these issues, Burgess and Spencer (2000) propose that pronunciation teaching methodology should be made the core aspect of the training and education of language teachers (TELT) courses. Likewise, it is well worth pursuing more research on L2 phonology acquisition and instruction since it can inform the development of pronunciation curriculums, as well as the design of pronunciation teaching materials and methodologies.

L2 phonology researchers have devoted a considerable amount of effort to unraveling the system of interlanguage phonology and the role of L1 in L2 pronunciation attainment (Setter & Jenkins, 2005). Another line of studies within pronunciation research comprises the investigation of predictors of pronunciation accuracy. Researchers in this area have examined the interplay among pronunciation accuracy and a realm of factors which has included age, length of residence in an L2-speaking country, degree of motivation, instruction, gender, desire to improve pronunciation, among others (see for example Purcell & Suter, 1980 and Piske, MacKay & Flege, 2001).

Pronunciation researchers have also advocated that phonology instruction should have as a primary aim improved intelligibility and this has naturally led to an increasing interest in endeavors that have implications for intelligibility and comprehensibility (see for example Derwing, 2008). These studies typically involve native-speaking raters who assess the pronunciation performance of L2 learners in areas that range from segmental and suprasegmental features to vowel quality, speech rate, and voicing. Derwing and Munro (2005, p. 381) claim that rating-judgment studies "have shown a high degree of reliability across groups of listeners, such that some shared sense of what constitutes intelligible versus unintelligible L2 speech is possible." An example of this subfield of L2 pronunciation research includes Scales *et al.*'s (2006) undertaking, whose findings indicate that L1/L2 users' speech rate directly affects the relationship between intelligibility and listener's accent preferences. They report that the Mexican accent, the fastest, with 180 words per minute, was the least preferred, while learners' favorite accent, the American, was in fact the slowest, with 147 words per minute.

Jenkins' (2000) *lingua franca core*, a proposal for intelligibility-based pronunciation instruction, shares the same concern for improved L2 intelligibility. In her research, she identified a list of features which are crucial in promoting intelligible pronunciation among non-native speaker interactions and, accordingly, she proposes that such features should be the focus of L2 pronunciation instruction[3].

Pronunciation pedagogy has also attracted the attention of SLA researchers whose studies suggest that pronunciation instruction can improve L2 learners' oral production. Curriculum issues and the integration of pronunciation in communicative teaching contexts have also been widely investigated (see for example Burgess & Spencer, 2000; Levis, 2005; Derwing, 2005 and Isaacs, 2009).

To conclude, although not a prominent research area in SLA, this review demonstrates that there has been an increasing interest among researchers on L2 pronunciation acquisition and instruction. Important aspects of the process involved in L2 pronunciation attainment, remain, however, unanswered.

2.2 *The socio-psychological dimension of L2 phonological attainment*

The research that will be reported in this section contributed to the design of the questionnaire of learner beliefs about ESL pronunciation. In order to understand the motivation as well as the rationale behind the questionnaire of pronunciation beliefs, I now turn to a consideration of socio-psychological aspects of L2 phonology acquisition, a scope of pronunciation studies that has been increasingly investigated from different perspectives.

---

[3] The features include "most consonant sounds, vowel quantity, initial and medial consonant clusters, and tonic stress" (Jenkins, 2004, p. 115).

In Ioup's (1989) oft-cited study, two immigrant children, namely a successful and an unsuccessful L2 learner, are contrasted in relation to their neurological profiles and aspects of grammar. The results are inconclusive as the study fails to provide an apparent explanation for the unsuccessful learner's failure in acquiring native-like proficiency in English. Ioup suggests that "there could be a degree of talent in language learning ability not related to other cognitive talents" (p. 170).

This study demonstrates that success in foreign language learning cannot be solely explained on the basis of linguistic and cognitive factors. In this respect,

Jilka (2009a, p. 10) claims that a neurologically based component such as age of learning onset is not a determining factor of L2 ability. He observes that "it is quite apparent that within groups of learners who acquire a certain L2 at roughly the same age, there will be some who perform better than others". This phenomenon indicates that the process of L2 acquisition is influenced not only by biological timetables, but also by learners' sociolinguistic profiles and their language attitudes, motivations, and identities (Levis, 2005; Jenkins, 2004).

In relation to the latter, Setter and Jenkins (2005, p. 5) explain that phonology is inseparably connected with identity since foreign accents are an expression of "how we want to be seen by others, of the social communities with which we identify or seek membership, and of whom we admire or ostracize". Smit (2002) observes that learners' feelings of identity are closely related to L2 pronunciation and, in similar vein, Levis (2005, p. 374, 375) proposes that "the role of identity in accent is perhaps as strong as the biological constraints".

In a study that investigated the relationship between ethnic group affiliation and L2 pronunciation attainment, Gatbonton, Trofimovich, and Magid (2005) found that learners perceive their peers' L2 accent as an indicator of their degree of affiliation to their home ethnic group. This experiment suggests that pronunciation inaccuracy may reflect social pressure from home communities or same-L1 peers rather than lack of aptitude or concern for pronunciation accuracy.

In addition, Levis (2005, p. 375) notes that L2 accented speech is particularly bound up with identity for non-native foreign language teachers. He examines that for these teachers pronunciation "may be a matter of pride or uneasiness". In a study of beliefs of Greek EFL instructors, Sifakis and Sougari (2005) provide paradoxical results. Despite recognizing that near-native accents are not the norm in communication between non-native speakers, these teachers reported that a near-native accent is the standard pronunciation model in their teaching contexts.

Considering that pronunciation may be the most emotionally loaded aspect of SLA (Baran-Łucarz, 2011), learner anxiety is another factor believed to play a central role on L2 phonology acquisition. In anxiety studies, a distinction is made between trait anxiety, which refers to a general predisposition to become anxious, and language anxiety, a uniquely L2-specific variable. Similarly, beneficial and debilitating anxiety are differentiated since in some situations anxiety can actually promote language performance (Léger & Storch, 2009). Dörnyei (2005, p. 201) examines that "we still have no clear theoretical understanding of the circumstances in which certain levels of language anxiety can be helpful". Despite this limitation, he also reports that relevant empirical studies within SLA have demonstrated that there is a moderate negative correlation between language anxiety and L2 performance.

In what regards the influence of language anxiety on L2 pronunciation ability, Guiora (1990 in Jilka, 2009a, p. 4) theorizes that phonological accuracy is influenced by the permeability of ego boundaries. Simply put, he claims that when the ego boundaries are weakened, L2 pronunciation improves. BaranŁucarz (2014) also posits that pronunciation anxiety is related to various constructs, such as pronunciation self-image, fear of negative evaluation, beliefs which are related to the importance attributed to L2 pronunciation, and pronunciation self-efficacy or self-assessment. Unsurprisingly, Szyszka's undertaking (2011) reports a significant relationship between foreign language anxiety and pronunciation self-assessment. In her study, more apprehensive teacher trainees declared lower pronunciation competence, while subjects with lower levels of anxiety perceived their pronunciation to be more successful.

Other studies have investigated the notions of self-efficacy, self-esteem and self-confidence. According to Dörnyei (2005, p. 211), these variables are related to learner beliefs about their attributes and abilities. While self-esteem and self-confidence comprise broader categories, self-efficacy beliefs consist of opinions about one's capabilities to perform certain tasks (Dörnyei, 2005) and have been linked to a number of factors, including strategy use (Macaro, 2013, p. 290), motivation (Smit, 2002, p. 95), and students' willingness to communicate in the target language (Léger & Storch, 2009, p. 270).

Furthermore, the view that it is difficult to assess one's own pronunciation is confirmed in Dlaska and Krekeler's (2008) study of L2 pronunciation self-assessment. Their findings reveal that although in 85% of all cases learners' self-assessments were reliable, a low level of agreement concerning inaccurate sounds was encountered. Learners' motivation to improve their pronunciation skills also appears to have a bearing on L2 phonological attainment. By way of illustration, Smit (2002) conducted an experiment which examined the interaction between a number of motivational factors and achievement in advanced EFL pronunciation learning. She correlated students' scores on pronunciation tests with the results from a self-devised motivation questionnaire. Her findings indicate that students who have a positive attitude towards pronunciation learning are more likely to pass a university pronunciation module. What is more, her correlations reveal that, ideally, learners should begin the module with an above-average proficiency, be self-confident, intrinsically motivated, and ready to work more independently and intensively. Similarly, Dalton and Smit (1997) and Moyer's (1999) endeavors provide findings that support the value of motivation in pronunciation acquisition. Moyer (1999) found that age is not an independent predictor of successful L2 phonological attainment, being confounded with two other contributing variables, namely motivation and pronunciation instruction.

Additionally, the field of language learning strategies, that is, "activities consciously chosen by learners for the purpose of regulating their own learning" (Griffiths, 2008, p. 87), has provided important contributions to generate a better understanding of the processes involved in L2 phonological acquisition. Language learning strategies seem to be particularly relevant to pronunciation instruction as the study of this skill is most profitable when learners are actively involved in their learning (Morley, 1991).

In a study which reports a discrepancy between recent research on L2 phonology and learners' perceptions of their pronunciation difficulties and strategies, Derwing and Rossiter (2002) reveal learners' preference of pronunciation strategies of low efficiency. The authors attribute these findings to a focus on segmental features in commercially available pronunciation materials, as well as teachers' lack of formal training in pronunciation instruction. However, an obvious caveat needs to be raised. Despite claiming that few studies have investigated pronunciation strategies, the majority of the strategies examined by the authors are not exclusively applicable to pronunciation and seem to be more generally related to communication. In any case, this study contributes to L2 pronunciation instruction as it informs teachers and material designers of learners' approaches to L2 phonology learning and it also emphasizes the need to teach learners more effective pronunciation learning strategies.

In 2011, Calka proposed a taxonomy of pronunciation learning strategies (PLS) which was grounded on her own study with Polish L1 students enrolled in teacher training pronunciation courses. Her findings reveal that although participants employed direct, indirect, and metacognitive PLS, their repertoire of strategies was not wide. Participants in this study reported that their most frequently used pronunciation strategies consist of rote learning, repeating after native-speakers, paying attention to pronunciation, and having a sense of humor about their own mispronunciations. Conversely, searching for information on phonetics and phonology books or websites is the least frequently deployed strategy among this group of learners.

Research on language attitudes is another popular subfield of pronunciation and individual difference (ID) studies. As previously mentioned, pronunciation is possibly the most sensitive area of language; therefore, it does not come as a surprise that this skill elicits strong attitudes. Gabillon (2007, p. 69) explains that attitudes involve positive or negative dispositions towards certain situations or behaviors. These attitudes towards L2 pronunciation acquisition and learning contribute to students' pronunciation learning preferences, goals, and even outcomes (Setter & Jenkins, 2005).

Two vigorous strands in this area of research consist of attitudes towards English as a Lingua Franca (ELF) and accent preference studies. An example of the former is Stanojevic, Borenic and Smojver's (2012) study of the attitudes of Croatian speakers towards pronunciation and ELF. Results are contradictory in view of participants declaring that pronunciation is important (89%) and agreeing that aiming for near-native pronunciation is a worthwhile endeavor (67%), while showing no concern for speaking with a strong accent to native-speakers (76.1%). In another ELF undertaking, Kaypak and Ortaçtepe (2014) were interested in whether Turkish exchange students' beliefs would change after study abroad sojourns in ELF contexts. It was found that overall participants' ELF attitudes remained the same. The researchers reported, however, that after the sojourns students emphasized the value of intelligibility among interactions in ELF environments (see also Meerleer, 2012).

In spite of this recent interest in ELF attitudes, accent preference studies remain the predominant area of inquiry in pronunciation attitudes research. An example of this line of research includes Ladegaard and Sachdev's (2006) analysis of attitudes of Danish EFL learners towards British and American varieties of English. The researchers reveal that despite embracing American culture, these learners demonstrate a desire to adopt a British accent (Received

Pronunciation). Dalton-Puffer, Kaltenboeck, and Smit (1997) report similar findings among Austrian EFL learners.

Few studies to date (e.g., Elliot, 1995 and Moyer, 2007) have attempted to investigate whether there is a relationship between phonological accuracy and attitudes towards L2 pronunciation.

Elliot (1995) analyzed the foreign-accented speech of 66 undergraduate L2 Spanish students in relation to 12 variables. The main aim of the study was to investigate the relationship among field independence, hemispheric specialization, pronunciation attitudes, and subjects' pronunciation accuracy of the target language. Other variables, however, were included to control for external factors which could relate to differences in pronunciation ability. With the exception of the first section of the test, pronunciation attitude was the most significant predictor of pronunciation accuracy.

The instrument employed to examine learners' pronunciation attitudes imposes a limitation to this study. Elliot's Pronunciation Attitude Inventory (PAI) consists of merely 12 items and, consequently, relevant conceptual elements that encompass attitudes towards L2 pronunciation are not included. Of the 12 items in Elliot's PAI, six relate to learners' concern for pronunciation accuracy, two items pertain to pronunciation learning goals, two comprise self-efficacy beliefs, one item concerns pronunciation learning strategies, and, finally, one single item involves attitudes towards pronunciation instruction.

As the vast majority of the items in Elliot's PAI concern learners' desire to improve their pronunciation, rather than a combination of positive attitudes towards pronunciation, his experiment reveals that concern for pronunciation accuracy is the single most significant factor affecting subjects' interlanguage phonology.

In the second study, Moyer (2007) sought to investigate the interplay between pronunciation and language attitudes and she found a relation between participants' degree of accentedness and language attitudes among 50 ESL subjects representing 15 nationalities. Moyer reports significant correlations between accent ratings and language attitudes. The latter comprised reasons for learning English, perceived ability to improve in English, desire to improve pronunciation, self-confidence, comfort with assimilation to the target language culture, and intention to reside long-term in an L2 speaking environment.

2.3 *An overview of learner beliefs*

In this section, I will provide a description of how researchers conceptualize learner beliefs about SLA and briefly review a common criticism in the field. Pedagogical implications of research on learner beliefs are also discussed.

Language learners hold strong assumptions about L2 language acquisition and instruction. Frequent learners' beliefs about SLA may include opinions about the nature of language learning and its degree of difficulty, effective learning strategies, whether language aptitude predisposes success, expectations and motivations, among others (Gregersen & MacIntyre, 2014, p. 33). These preconceived ideas generally reflect students' cultural backgrounds and their previous experiences in L2 contexts (Kalaja & Barcelos, 2003).

Research in the field of SLA demonstrates that students' perceptions about language learning seem to have a powerful impact on L2 acquisition as learners interpret their language learning experiences and behave in L2 learning contexts in light of the assumptions they hold (White, 2008; Brown, 2009). According to Riley (1997, in Kalaja & Barcelos, 2003, p. 8), teachers, researchers, and theoretical linguists need to value learners' subjective reality as students' theories, rather than anybody else's, play a crucial role on their learning.

Similarly, teachers' beliefs exert a significant effect on their classroom behaviors and instructional decisions, and, consequently, their views affect students' learning outcomes (Fang, 1996 and Gob & Chen, 2014). Gregersen and MacIntyre (2014) analyze that teachers can make more informed decisions concerning their instructional practices provided that they reflect about their own beliefs about SLA. By the same token, modifying teachers' counterproductive beliefs will result in genuine and effective change in teachers' behaviors.

Horwitz (1985) introduced language learner beliefs into the L2 literature with a research paper in which she describes the Beliefs About Language Learning Inventory (BALLI), a Likert-scale questionnaire that has been extensively employed to investigate teachers' and learners' preconceived ideas about language learning. The BALLI was exhaustively applied to beliefs studies and thus proved to be an important contribution to the field. Other methods have been employed in the beliefs literature. Barcelos (2014) reports that common forms of data collection include classroom observations, interviews, simulated recalls, open-ended questionnaires, metaphors, and multimedia narratives.

Tse (2000), for example, examined the perceptions of 51 adult FL learners with the unprecedented use in beliefs research of learners' autobiographies. Her qualitative analysis of students' writings provided three categories of data, which include classroom interactions, perceived level of success, and attributions of success and failure. Tse's data reveals that these learners believe they have low levels of proficiency. What is more, they also reported that their instruction should be more focused on oral communication, and they tended to attribute their failures in acquiring a FL to their lack of effort.

In what was an atypical experiment within this strand of SLA research, Rieger (2009) examined the role of target language and gender in shaping learner beliefs. She found that these two variables led to significant differences in the beliefs about SLA held by her participants, first-year English and German students at a university in Budapest. It was more common among German majors to view their target language as difficult. These learners were also more inclined to agree that traditional approaches to language learning, such as the translation method and an emphasis on grammar, were useful. With regard to gender, the only statistically significant difference that was found refers to the perceived importance of certain language learning approaches or techniques. Female learners in this study were more prone to agree that traditional approaches are important to language learning.

Studies on beliefs about second language acquisition have emphasized L2 teachers and learners' general assumptions about language and language learning (see Fang, 1996). Researchers have also addressed the relation between learners' perceptions and strategy use (see for example Cotterall, 1995 and Yang, 1999), mismatches between teacher and learner beliefs (see for example Holec, 1987 and Brown, 2009), and the influence of learning context on learner beliefs (Horwitz, 1999).

Despite having provided these contributions to L2 research and instruction, the field of learner beliefs is treated with skepticism by certain ID researchers. Among them, Dörnyei (2005) is particularly reluctant to accept that learner's perceptions about SLA constitute a proper ID variable. In spite of recognizing that knowledge systems affect learning behavior, he claims that beliefs are not an "enduring, trait-like factor" (p. 214). He also argues that its taxonomy is open and that it can include related and 'well-established' ID categories, such as language attitudes and self-confidence perceptions, which prevent us from identifying a closed system of beliefs. However, Dörnyei's criticism seems contradictory seeing that he also recommends future researchers to broaden the theoretical basis of learner beliefs.

Nevertheless, beliefs about SLA may have significant implications for instruction. Although some long-held views may be less malleable and "more stubbornly embraced than others" (Gregersen & MacIntyre, 2014, p. 32), Kalaja and Barcelos (2003, p. 233) posit that beliefs are dynamic and emergent. Therefore, practitioners and material designers can address learner beliefs that seem to be detrimental to L2 acquisition and instruction in order to enhance educational effectiveness. Finally, we still lack an understanding of the extent to which learner beliefs about L2 learning relate to ultimate attainment in a foreign language. For these reasons, research on beliefs about SLA continues to be a worthwhile endeavor.

2.4 Learner beliefs about L2 pronunciation

Research that has attempted to investigate learner beliefs about L2 pronunciation is scant (e.g., Deneckere, 2011; Müller, 2011; Waniek--Klimczak; 2011; Van Schoor, 2010; Simon, 2005 and Sobkowiak, 2002). Relevant studies in this area of research include Cenoz and Lecumberi (1999) and Simon and Taveniers' (2011) undertakings, which examine learners' general perceptions of factors that influence the acquisition of L2 pronunciation.

Cenoz and Lecumberi (1999) analyzed learners' awareness of English segmental and suprasegmental features as well as their accent preferences and perceptions of the difficulty or ease of understanding English accents. The authors investigated the differences in beliefs about factors that influence the acquisition of English pronunciation of 86 university students from two linguistic groups, that is, Basque L1 learners and Spanish L1 learners. The results of the study reveal that pronunciation is considered to be a difficult, yet important skill. Learners also regard contact with native speakers and phonetic training as the most influential factors in the acquisition of pronunciation. The findings also indicate that there are no significant differences in the factors that are perceived by both linguistic groups as most influential in the acquisition of English phonology.

Simon and Taverniers' (2011) study makes interesting contributions towards a better understanding of students' perspectives on the acquisition of L2 phonology. Contrary to Cenoz and Lecumberri' (1999) findings, participants in this undertaking, 117 L1 Dutch learners in Flanders, consider pronunciation the easiest component when learning L2 English. In addition, according to these learners, the most efficient pronunciation learning method is a one-year stay in an English speaking country, followed by in-class exercises and self-study. They also believe that high levels of phonological attainment are associated with 'talent'. Finally, 96% of participants reported that they aim for a near-native English pronunciation.

Simon and Taveniers' study would have been somewhat more relevant if the EFL context where this research was conducted accounted for most EFL realities. The researchers recognize that their participants, young and middleaged EFL speakers in Flanders, are generally highly proficient in English. Results of a study on learner beliefs about English pronunciation where the percentage of high proficiency in English is lower will certainly differ from their findings.

Their results suggest that learning context exerts a strong influence on the construction of learner beliefs about L2 pronunciation. A few SLA researchers have, in fact, investigated the interplay between learning context and pronunciation beliefs.

An example of this line of research includes Nowacka's (2012) undertaking, which provides a cross-cultural perspective of L2 pronunciation beliefs. She examines the beliefs of Italian, Spanish, and Polish L1 learners of English and her findings suggest that the group of Italian L1 learners is the least likely to study pronunciation outside the language classroom. In relation to pronunciation strategies, despite 'listening to authentic English' being the preferred strategy for all the examined nationalities, the pronunciation strategies of these three groups of learners differ considerably. Italians, for example, regard 'primary and secondary school education' the second most beneficial means of acquiring L2 pronunciation, while the Spanish ranked 'contacts with native speaker' and 'practical phonetics' as their second preferred strategies, and, lastly, the Poles believe 'practical phonetics', 'imitating authentic speech', and 'contacts with native speakers' are the second most influential factors on the acquisition of English pronunciation.

Clearly, the lack of undertakings in the area of beliefs about L2 pronunciation suggests the need for more studies. In the same fashion, this strand of SLA research would benefit from the design of a comprehensive taxonomy of L2 learners' pronunciation beliefs, which could subsequently be applied in studies with distinct populations. Finally, few studies to date have investigated whether there is a relationship between L2 phonological accuracy and pronunciation beliefs. Accordingly, the caveats that have been raised as well as the lack of studies call for more research in this area.

2.5 *Studies of successful phonological attainment*

Bongaerts, Planken and Schils (1995) examined the commonly held notion that, as opposed to adults, children are very successful L2 language learners when it comes to the acquisition of accent. They were interested in establishing whether late learners who show mastery of an L2 phonological system could pass for a native speaker of that target language. The speech samples of 22 subjects, that is, L1 Dutch learners who had started to learn English at around the age of 12, were judged by four native speakers of British English with no experience in pronunciation assessment. In addition, a control group of 5 native speakers of British English was included. The researchers report surprising results: (a) the average score assigned to the group of native speakers was quite low and (b) 10 highly successful learners outperformed the group of native speakers. It should be noted that subjects in this study consisted of very advanced learners of English who had received intensive pronunciation instruction at university. In any case, the findings from this study indicate that there appear to be cases of late L2 learners who can pass for native speakers. These results also suggest that phonology instruction can have a significant impact on learners' interlanguage phonology.

In another experiment that contributes towards a better understanding of L2 phonological success, Piller (2002) provides a description of high-level L2 pronunciation attainment through the accounts of successful L1 German users of English. She reports that in these accounts passing for a native speaker was a measurement of high achievement among expert L2 speakers and, accordingly, her research focuses on her subjects' passing practices. 27 out of

73 participants in this study mentioned they could pass for native speakers in certain contexts. Her data also shows that high-level achievement in the L2 may be audience-specific, that is, her subjects reflected that their linguistic performance varies perceptively with distinct interlocutors.

Furthermore, because L2 users in this study were married to native speakers of English, Piller's experiment suggests that amount of use of the target language may be related to pronunciation accuracy. What is more, learners' motivation and agency seem to be crucial factors contributing to ultimate attainment. In accordance with the previous study, age in this experiment cannot be claimed to be a predictor of pronunciation accuracy.

In an attempt to determine which ID variables lead to success in L2 pronunciation, Baran--Łucarz (2007) provides detailed profiles of 3 'excellent', 5 'very good' and 5 'very poor' learners in this aspect of foreign language attainment. The researcher conducted a rating-judgment study, which allowed her to classify learners in the three categories. Additionally, subjects completed a questionnaire about their background as L2 English learners and their cognitive preferences were diagnosed. Results reveal that 'excellent' pronunciation learners show a strong concern for pronunciation accuracy, are intrinsically motivated, believe they have control over their pronunciation, are Field Independent learners, and have an innate gift for music.

Conversely, 'very poor' pronunciation learners in this study have no musical talent, and believe they are unable to control their ability to achieve successful phonological attainment. Surprisingly, these learners also show great concern for pronunciation accuracy, and consider their phonetic knowledge 'quite good'. Baran-Łucarz hypothesizes that learners' false picture of their own skills may negatively affect their achievements. Her findings also suggest that cognitive traits seem to be the most crucial variables when it comes to phonological success. However, these results need to be treated with caution seeing that most factors investigated in this experiment were cognitive.

Lastly, in a theoretical undertaking, Brown (2008) describes the relationship between L2 pronunciation and research on good language learners. His article, however, receives little support from research since few investigators have attempted to examine how language learners arrive at pronunciation accuracy. Brown only mentions Purcell and Suter's (1980) often-quoted research, which investigates the variables that seem to influence success in L2 phonology. This study consisted of 14 judges, who rated the pronunciation accuracy of 61 non-native speakers of English. The results show that aptitude of oral mimicry was the most significant factor on the success of L2 pronunciation, followed by length of time in an English-speaking country and/or living with a native speaker, and strength of concern for pronunciation accuracy.

In conclusion, contrary to the long-held notion that late learners are incapable of achieving high levels of L2 pronunciation attainment, these studies suggest that, albeit the minority, there appear to be cases of successful phonological acquisition among L2 late learners. These experiments also demonstrate that a number of variables that may predict learners' interlanguage phonology have been underexplored. Similarly, the subfield of successful phonological attainment, much like research on L2 phonology, has not received considerable attention. This type of research merits further investigation since it can contribute towards a better understanding of how learners arrive at pronunciation accuracy, which may, in turn, eventually assist in the development of pedagogical materials and classroom practices aimed at improving learners' phonological skills.

2.6 *Conclusions*

The existing literature on second language acquisition remains insufficient to provide an accurate understanding of what is involved in successful attainment of an L2 phonological system. The area of socio-psychological aspects involved in pronunciation acquisition is particularly underresearched. Within this area, beliefs about second language learning and acquisition appear to be closely related to phonological attainment in view of pronunciation being the most sensitive aspect of SLA, and as such it can engender strong attitudes and beliefs. Therefore, the present study focuses on beliefs which L2 learners hold about pronunciation attainment. It is of particular interest the influence of pronunciation beliefs on phonological performance, constituting a topic which has not been often addressed in the beliefs research.

Chapter Three

PREDICTORS OF L2 PHONOLOGICAL PERFORMANCE – THE CASE OF BRAZILIAN ESL LEARNERS

This chapter presents an account of the instruments employed in the study reported in this book, the procedures involved in data collection, as well as a description of the methods of analysis adopted in the investigation. It also describes the questionnaire design and includes a brief overview of rating-judgment studies, that is, the method of pronunciation assessment employed in the research.

3.1 *Population and Sample*

This book surveys the impact of beliefs about L2 pronunciation on the interlanguage phonology of Brazilian ESL learners. The population includes Brazilian learners who study in the UK or subjects who have previously received formal instruction in English in the UK, but who are no longer studying. Participants were recruited voluntarily through language schools and personal referrals. A total of 30 respondents, 14 males and 16 females, ranging from 18 to 55 years of age participated in the study. All subjects were late learners, with the majority (53.4%) having started to learn English in primary or secondary school.

At the time of the study 9 respondents (30 %) had resided in the UK for more than 10 years, 6 (20%) had lived in England from 4 to 6 years, and 7 speakers (23.3%) had been living in England for less than 6 months. In relation to amount of continued L1 use, nearly half of participants (46.7%) reported that they frequently spoke Portuguese in the UK. Furthermore, 2 subjects (6.7%) had lived in another ESL environment for 4 to 6 years and 1 learner (3.3%) had resided in an English speaking country other than England for 1 to 3 years. Prior to participating in this study, none of the respondents had taken an English pronunciation course.

3.2 *Questionnaire Design*

For the purposes of the present research, a questionnaire of pronunciation beliefs about SLA was constructed. The first two parts of the questionnaire (see Appendix 3) consist of 6-point Likert-scale items pertaining to beliefs about L2 pronunciation acquisition and instruction, emotional beliefs, the dimension of status in pronunciation attainment, self-confidence beliefs, pronunciation learning goals, pronunciation learning strategies, and degree of social and cultural affiliation with the target language community (items 1-39). The three remaining parts include items referring to respondents' factual information, their pronunciation self--ratings, and learners' commentaries on the ways phonology is addressed in their English courses (items 40-49). For reasons of accessibility and practicality, a closed-response format was selected.

Following Dörnyei's (2013) proposal of an approach to ID research which does not isolate ID components, but rather validates interconnected learner characteristics, the present taxonomy for beliefs about L2 pronunciation combines variables that have been associated in the literature with learner beliefs (see section 2.2). Due to the complex nature of learner beliefs (Kalaja & Barcelos, 2003) and the absence of 'pure' individual difference (ID) factors (Dörnyei, 2013), I devised a questionnaire of pronunciation beliefs which integrates interrelated ID factors, including learner attitudes, language anxiety, motivation, willingness to communicate, self--confidence beliefs, and language learning strategies.

Additionally, existing inventories of learner beliefs (Horwitz, 1985; Cotterall, 1995; Sobkowiak, 2002; Cenoz & Lecumberri, 2005; Rieger, 2009; Kang, 2010; Simon & Taverniers, 2011; Meerleer, 2012; Kaypak & Ortaçtepe, 2014) were examined and appropriate items were modified to suit the context of this research. In the appendix (part 4) the source of each item is indicated.

The questionnaire was administered in Portuguese (see Appendix 2) and comprised eight constructs, namely, beliefs about pronunciation acquisition (items 1-4), beliefs about pronunciation instruction (items 5-8), emotional beliefs (items 9-12), functional beliefs (items 13-16), self-confidence beliefs (items 17-21), pronunciation learning goals (items 22-27), pronunciation learning strategies (items 28-32), and cultural beliefs (items 33-39).

Furthermore, nine negatively worded items (3, 10, 11, 12, 20, 25, 26, 27, and 37) were reverse coded before the scores were computed.

A pilot study was conducted with 18 respondents and the instrument reliability was verified statistically. Items 2, 8, 28 and 33 were removed and analysis using IBM SPSS Statistics 22.0 revealed a final Cronbach's Alpha reliability coefficient of .70. In addition, satisfactory inter-item correlations ($\alpha > .60$) were achieved for all constructs, except for the trait of pronunciation learning goals, which was excluded from the analysis.

3.3 Rating-judgment study

Rating scales have been extensively employed in SLA research as an instrument within which human raters score L2 users' oral performance. Such assessment schemes structure raters' judgments through a fixed number of scale bands and enable researchers to quantify learners' degree of foreign accentedness (Isaacs & Thompson, 2013). Generally, only scalar endpoints are defined, with one end of the numerical rating scale being reserved for the category of "native-like pronunciation" or "not accented at all", while the other end is marked as "heavy foreign accent" or "definite foreign accent". The numbers between the two endpoints represent degrees of foreign accent within these two extremes (Piske et al., 2001).

Examples of variables or correlations which have been investigated under this research method include comprehensibility and intelligibility (see for example Munro & Derwing, 1995; Derwing & Munro, 1997; Major et al., 2002), fluency (see for example Rossiter, 2009), accent perceptions (see for example Scales et al., 2006), the interplay among pronunciation accuracy and cognitive, affective, and instructional factors (see for example Bongaerts et al., 1995; Moyer, 1999; Piske et al., 2001), and the relationship between learner attitudes and phonological attainment (see for example Elliot, 1995 and Pullen, 2012).

3.3.1 *Raters*

In relation to individuals who serve as judges in rating stimuli, McDermott (1986 in Jesney, 2004) examined a number of their distinguishing factors and concluded that the backgrounds of judges may affect the criteria they decide to adopt in rating individual speakers. Thus, it would seem that an important methodological consideration concerns the experience of the listeners who rate speech materials for degree of foreign accentedness.

ESL teachers, phoneticians or individuals with a certain degree of exposure to L2 speech have been classified in the literature as experienced. Novice raters, in turn, are often recruited to evaluate speech samples and comprise linguistically untrained listeners with limited familiarity with L2 speech (Piske et al., 2001 and Jesney, 2004).

Isaacs and Thompson (2013) report that there is no consensus in the literature regarding the employment of expert and naive raters. In an attempt to address the lack of agreement in the field, they examined the effects of rater experience on judgments of L2 pronunciation and their results revealed that experienced, i.e., ESL teachers, and novice raters arrived at virtually identical scoring decisions. Likewise, untrained raters in Derwing, Thomson and Munro's (2006) study were able to make statistically reliable judgments of short speech extracts. In addition to these findings, novice raters are a particularly attractive choice for rating-judgment studies since they represent the people with whom L2 users are likely to interact in real-world settings (Isaacs & Thompson, 2013).

For the purposes of the present study and in light of research which demonstrates that inexperienced native speakers can reliably judge L2 accented speech, linguistically untrained raters were selected.

The raters (2 males and 1 female) comprised three native speakers of English representing distinct L1 backgrounds (American, English, and Irish).

Their ages varied from 25 to 30 and all of them claimed to have experience as L2 users (French, German, and Irish, respectively). All raters reported a low degree of familiarity with spoken English of Brazilian speakers.

The judges' scores were analyzed statistically to determine their interrater reliability and a Cronbach's Alpha coefficient of .91 revealed a high degree of agreement among their ratings.

3.3.2 *Scale*

In assessing degrees of foreign accent, Jesney (2004) reports that researchers advocate the use of 9 or 11-point numerical rating scales due to the conclusion that smaller scales may cause a ceiling effect. Scales of 9 levels are, in fact, increasingly becoming a research convention in L2 pronunciation research (Isaacs & Thomsom, 2013). In order to make results comparable to other studies, it was decided to use in this study a 9-point numerical rating scale.

Raters were instructed that a score of 9 indicated that the subject's pronunciation of the target language was 'not accented at all'. A score of 5 represented a 'noticeable foreign accent', and a score of 1 meant that the individual had very little mastery of the target language phonological system and at times was almost unintelligible.

3.3.3 *Stimuli*

The types of elicitation techniques employed in studies of global foreign accentedness have varied considerably. Reading tasks of a fixed set of materials have been a common type of stimuli in accentedness judgments, and have included sentence-length (see for example Bongaerts *et al.*, 1995), paragraph-length (see for example Moyer, 1999) and word-length tokens (see for example Elliot, 1995).

Subjects have also been asked in a number of studies to recount personal experiences (see for example Pullen, 2012) or to describe pictures (see for example Isaacs & Thomson, 2013), thus producing samples of natural extemporaneous L2 speech which, in turn, provide judges with a more authentic representation of speakers' L2 oral performance. Yet, Jilka (2009b) examines that in free-response tasks participants may use avoidance strategies with regard to problematic L2 sounds, words or sentence structures, which can reduce the reliability of the evaluation. It would seem, then, that a combination of extemporaneous and read speech is the most effective technique in eliciting nonnative speech samples. In the present study, the elicitation techniques involved two reading tasks of word-level and sentence-level items, followed by a free-response task (see Appendix 5).

The selection of tokens for the first two tasks was grounded on studies of contrasts between the phonological systems of English and Brazilian Portuguese (Azevedo, 1981; Baptista, 2000; Kluge, 2004; Bettoni-Techio & Koerich, 2006; Reis, 2006; Cardoso, 2007; Osborne, 2008; Brawerman-Albini & Becker, 2014; Perozzo & Alves, 2014). An emphasis was given to Brazilian Portuguese phonotactic constraints (e.g., *special, feminism, pool, beat*), vowel and consonant conflations (e.g., *think, apple, girl, rap*), lexical stress position (e.g., *insight, envelope*), intonation patterns (e.g., *I didn't talk to Peter, I talked to Mary*), palatalization of final alveolar stops (e.g., *they never greet each other, I read easy books*), and vowel epenthesis in both word and sentence level productions (e.g., *worked, Internet, the cat went to the park, the road sign is green*).

The third technique was taken from Moyer (1999) and it consisted of a spontaneous speech task in which subjects were asked to recount personal experiences. In addition, according to Derwing (2008), the predictability of grammatical structures and vocabulary is a factor that appears to interact with L2 accent in judgment ratings. Thus, an attempt was made to include words and structures that were likely to be known by learners.

3.4 *Procedures*

Participants performed the rating-judgment tasks after questionnaire completion. The program Audacity 2.0.4 was used to normalize the speech samples and initial dysfluencies such as false starts and hesitations were excluded. Judges listened to the whole recording of the first two tasks, but were only exposed to extracts from the free-response task samples of an average of 14 seconds. Clips containing as few grammatical errors or filler utterances as possible were selected in order to control the pronunciation rating experiment. The extracts were then randomized and converted into mp3 files. Finally, the rating sessions lasted approximately 1 hour and 30 minutes and were arranged with each rater individually.

Chapter Four

EXAMINING THE IMPACT OF BELIEFS ABOUT PRONUNCIATION ON L2 PHONOLOGICAL PERFORMANCE

In this chapter I will present the results from the analysis. First, the statistical qualities of the data are provided. Next, findings from the correlations between constructs and mean ratings are reported, followed by a description of statistically relevant correlations between individual items and outcome. I then discuss learners' self-assessments and their relationship to raters' judgments.

Finally, significant findings for demographic variables are reported.

4.1 *Data Analysis*

The data was statistically analyzed using IBM SPSS Statistics 22. Satisfactory reliability estimates ($\alpha > .60$) were achieved for the seven constructs and a Cronbach's Alpha reliability coefficient of .64 was obtained for the scale. I hypothesize that the reliability value for the scale's internal consistency did not fall within the conventional range of .70 to .90 due to the hybridity of the variable being measured. Nevertheless, Nunnally (1978) indicates that an alpha value of .60 is accepted for newly-developed measures. For the above reasons, the instrument was found to be reliable.

A Shapiro-Wilk's test ($p > .05$ for each of the 39 items) and a visual inspection of histograms, normal Q-Q plots and box plots revealed that subjects' mean ratings were normally distributed for questionnaire scores. Thus, Pearson-Product Moment correlation analyses were performed with subjects' mean ratings on the pronunciation tasks and their mean scores on questionnaire items. In addition, bivariate correlations were computed for learners' pronunciation self-ratings and judges' assessments. In order to determine possible confounding factors, pronunciation ratings were also correlated with language background variables.

4.2 *Pronunciation mean scores*

Inspection of Table 4.1 reveals that participants received medium scores on the pronunciation test (individual means range from 2.21 to 7.44, with a group mean of 4.61). Given that raters scored learners' degree of accentedness on a 9-point numerical scale in which 9 represented 'not accented at all' and 1 indicated that the individual had very little mastery of the L2 phonological system, the table shows that few participants achieved high scores on the pronunciation test.

Table 4.1 Participants' mean ratings

Participant	Task 1 M	Task 2 M	Task 3 M	M
1	5.66	4.33	5.33	5.10
2	4.00	3.66	3.00	3.55
3	2.00	1.66	3.66	2.44
4	2.33	3.33	3.00	2.88
5	2.33	1.66	2.66	2.21
6	3.66	3.66	5.33	4.21
7	3.66	6.66	4.33	4.88
8	3.33	6.00	4.33	4.55
9	1.66	2.00	3.66	2.44
10	2.33	2.66	4.00	2.99
11	3.00	2.66	2.00	2.55
12	7.00	7.66	4.66	6.44
13	7.00	8.00	7.33	7.44

Participant	Task 1 M	Task 2 M	Task 3 M	M
14	3.33	4.33	5.66	4.44
15	3.66	6.33	7.66	5.88
16	4.00	5.00	6.66	5.22
17	4.33	3.66	5.66	4.55
18	5.00	5.66	7.33	5.99
19	5.66	5.33	7.00	5.99
20	6.33	6.66	7.33	6.77
21	4.66	5.33	4.66	4.88
22	5.00	4.33	6.33	5.22
23	7.33	7.00	7.33	7.22
24	4.33	3.66	5.33	4.44
25	3.33	3.00	5.66	3.99
26	5.00	5.33	5.66	5.33
27	3.66	2.33	3.33	3.10
28	6.00	5.00	6.00	5.66
29	4.33	2.00	6.00	4.11
30	2.66	4.33	4.66	3.88

Source: Author

4.3 *Beliefs about pronunciation: significant construct correlations*

Descriptive statistics were computed for all questionnaire items. Means, ranges, and standard deviations for items under the construct of emotional beliefs are reported in Table 4.2.

Table 4.2 Descriptive Statistics for emotional beliefs

Item	M	SD	Range
10."I feel insecure about my English pronunciation."	3.4	1.5	1-6
11."My pronunciation improves when I speak with non-native speakers."	3.1	1.7	1-6
12."I feel less anxious when I speak with non-native speakers of English."	3.6	1.4	1-6

Note. Strongly Agree = 1 ; Agree = 2 ; Slightly Agree = 3 ; Slightly Disagree = 4 ; Disagree = 5; Strongly Disagree = 6.

Source: Author

As the figures indicate, in general participants declared moderate to low levels of pronunciation inhibition and anxiety. A Pearson Product Moment correlation analysis revealed a moderate negative relationship between the construct of emotional beliefs and learners' mean pronunciation scores in each rating- judgment task, r= -.50, p = .007, p < .01 for task 1, r= -.40, p = .038, p < .05 for task 2, and r= -.41, p= 032, p < .05 for task 3. The negative correlations indicate that students who declared lower levels of pronunciation anxiety were likely to be more successful at the phonological component of the target language.

Table 4.3 summarizes descriptives for the items under the construct of self-confidence beliefs.

Table 4.3 Descriptive Statistics for self-confidence beliesfs

Item	M	SD	Range
17."I think I have foreign language aptitude (a special ability for learning foreign languages)."	3.8	1.1	1-6
18."I believe I can eventually speak English very well."	5.5	.68	4-6
19." I am happy with my present English pronunciation."	4.1	1.3	2-6
21."Sometimes I can pass for a native speaker in brief interactions.	2.4	1.2	1-6

Note. Strongly Agree = 6 ; Agree = 5 ; Slightly Agree = 4 ; Slightly Disagree = 3 ; Disagree = 2; Strongly Disagree = 1.

Source: Author

From Table 4.3 it can be seen that although few participants declared to have experienced passing practices (see Piller, 2002, section 2.5), learners were predominantly optimistic about their pronunciation skills.

After correlation computations were performed, self-confidence beliefs and pronunciation performance results were found to be statistically significant, r = .39, p = .032, p < .05, r = .38, p = .039, p < .05, and r = .36, p = .053, p > .05 for tasks 1, 2, and 3, respectively. Although the null hypothesis cannot be rejected for task 3, it can be concluded from these results that there is a marginally significant correlation between subjects' ratings in task 3 and their self-confidence beliefs (p = .053, p > .05). In addition, the analysis revealed a moderate positive relationship between self-confidence beliefs and learners' mean pronunciation scores, r = .42, p = .022, p < .05. These findings indicate that participants who obtained high scores on judges' ratings seem to be more confident with their foreign accent. In other words, the correlation analyses demonstrate that positive attitudes towards self-perceived pronunciation performance are associated with higher levels of pronunciation attainment.

4.4 *Beliefs about pronunciation: significant item correlations*

Bivariate correlations also revealed significant relationships between individual questionnaire items and mean pronunciation scores (see Appendix 7 for non-significant item correlations). Results for the interplay between item 4 and mean ratings are given in Table 4.4.

Table 4.4 "It is best to learn English in an English speaking country."

Accent ratings	r	p	Sig. (2-tailed)
Task 1	-.47	.010	.05
Task 2	-.50	.005	.01
Task 3	-.13	.501	.05
Mean	-.48	.007	.01

Source: Author

No significant correlations were found between item 4 and judgment ratings on task 3, r= -.13, p > .05. However, it can be seen from Table 4.4 that the item "it is best to learn English in an English speaking country" exerted a significant negative effect on mean ratings, r= -48, p < .01. The analysis demonstrates that learners with lower degrees of foreign accent do not seem to agree that stays abroad are the most effective strategy in achieving success in a foreign language.

Table 4.5 displays the correlations between item 6 and scores received on the pronunciation test.

Table 4.5 "I would take a pronunciation course if it were available to me."

Accent ratings	r	p	Sig. (2-tailed)
Task 1	-.21	.267	.05
Task 2	-.51	.004	.01
Task 3	-.43	.018	.05
Mean	-.42	.022	.05

Source: Author

The item "I would take a pronunciation course if it were available to me" was significantly related to all sections of the pronunciation test except for task 1, the word repetition exercise. These results suggest that students with higher pronunciation scores seem to be satisfied with their own phonological performance and, accordingly, demonstrate a lack of investment in pronunciation training. This significant correlation appears to be consonant with the previous finding that self-confidence beliefs are conducive to higher levels of pronunciation attainment (see section 4.3).

Table 4.6 "I feel at ease when I have to speak English."

Accent ratings	r	p	Sig. (2-tailed)
Task 1	.45	.011	.05
Task 2	.52	.003	.01
Task 3	.71	.001	.01
Mean	.57	.001	.01

Source: Author

As seen in Table 4.6, statistical tests revealed a moderate positive correlation between outcome and the item "I feel at ease when I have to speak English", r = .57, p < .01. This relationship reinforces the finding that low levels of pronunciation anxiety and embarrassment contribute to pronunciation accuracy (see section 4.3). Furthermore, the analysis revealed a moderate negative correlation for learners' mean ratings and the items "I feel insecure about my pronunciation", r = -.58, p = .001, p < .01 and "my pronunciation improves when I speak with non-native speakers", r = -.47, p = .008, p < .01, thus indicating that subjects with high pronunciation scores share low levels of pronunciation anxiety. These findings are consonant with results reported in Table 4.6 and strengthen the negative correlation between emotional beliefs and L2 pronunciation performance.

Likewise, the aforementioned results are in accord with the positive relationship that was revealed between outcome and the construct of self-confidence beliefs. In relation to the latter, correlations were found for the items "I am happy with my present pronunciation", r = .64, p = .000, p < .01 and "my English pronunciation is below the average", r = -.45, p = .012, p < .05. These findings suggest that learners with low degrees of foreign accented speech seem to be confident about their phonological skills, and such confidence may well account for their self-reported low levels of pronunciation anxiety.

4.5 Beliefs about pronunciation: non-significant construct correlations

In this section I report descriptive statistics for items under constructs which did not demonstrate significance for mean rating results. Means, ranges, and standard deviations for the construct of beliefs about pronunciation acquisition are reported in Table 4.7.

Table 4.7 Descriptive Statistics for beliesfs about pronunciation acquisition

Item	M	SD	Range
1."It is easier for children than adults to use correct pronunciation."	5.1	1.1	1-6
3."Your proficiency in English pronunciation depends on factors you have little control over."	2.8	1.4	1-6
4."It is best to learn English pronunciation in an English speaking country."	5.5	1.2	1-6

Note. Strongly Agree = 6 ; Agree = 5 ; Slightly Agree = 4 ; Slightly Disagree = 3 ; Disagree = 2; Strongly Disagree = 1 for items 1 and 4; Strongly Agree = 1 ; Agree = 2 ; Slightly Agree = 3 ; Slightly Disagree = 4 Disagree = 5 ; Strongly Disagree = 6 for item 3.

Source: Author

Although the construct of beliefs about pronunciation acquisition was not found to be a predictor of outcome (r = -.25, p = .19), the analysis revealed a moderate negative relationship between the item "It is best to learn English pronunciation in an English speaking country" and mean ratings (see section 4.4).

Overall, participants reported that pronunciation accuracy is related to factors they cannot control. The majority of learners, for example, believes age of first exposure to the target language is associated with higher levels of phonological performance. Curiously, most respondents also agreed that pronunciation instruction should be included in ESL classes, and many noted that they would take a pronunciation course. As can be seen in Table 4.8, a large number of learners also subscribes to the view that phonetic symbols can enhance their phonological skills in the target language. These conflicting findings indicate that in spite of sharing the view that they have little control over their performance in the L2 pronunciation, learners also believe that they should not be deprived of phonological instruction.

Table 4.8 Descriptive Statistics for beliefs about pronunciation instruction

Item	M	SD	Range
5."Pronunciation instruction should be included in English classes."	5.6	6.1	4.6
6." I would take pronunciation course if available	4.5	1.4	1.6
7. "Learning phonetic symbols English can improve pronunciation".	4.5	1.3	2.6

Note. Strongly Agree = 6 ; Agree = 5 ; Slightly Agree = 4 ; Slightly Disagree = 3 ; Disagree = 2; Strongly Disagree = 1.

Source: Author

Furthermore, with the exception of the item "I would take a pronunciation course if it were available to me" (see section 4.4), no significant correlations were found for beliefs about pronunciation instruction, $r = -.20$, $p = .29$. Similarly, beliefs concerning the status of successful mastery of the L2 phonological system did not relate significantly to mean ratings, $r = -.08$, $p = .67$. Table 4.9 gives the descriptives for items under this construct.

Table 4.9 Descriptive Statistics for functional beliefs

Item	M	SD	Range
13."Having a good pronunciation in English is important for my professional career."	5.2	.84	3-6
14."Having a good pronunciation in English will permit me to become an influential member of my community."	4.4	1.3	2-6

| 15. "A good pronunciation in English will allow me to interact more easily with native speakers of English." | 5.4 | .85 | 3-6 |
| 16. "A good pronunciation in English will allow me to interact more easily with speakers who do not speak my language." | 5.0 | .86 | 3-6 |

Note. Strongly Agree = 6 ; Agree = 5 ; Slightly Agree = 4 ; Slightly Disagree = 3 ; Disagree = 2; Strongly Disagree = 1.

Source: Author

On the whole, participants shared the view that higher levels of pronunciation attainment are conducive to societal and professional success. However, these beliefs were not predictors of outcome. Likewise, pronunciation learning strategies were not significantly related to learners' pronunciation ratings, r = .12, p = .51. As can be seen from Table 4.10, the majority of respondents agreed that it is important to be actively involved in the process of L2 pronunciation learning.

Table 4.10 Descriptive Statistics for pronunciation learning strategies

Item	M	SD	Range
29. "I pay attention to how people pronounce words in English."	5.2	.81	3-6
30. "I pay attention to rhythm and intonation when other people speak English."	5.0	.98	3-6
31. "I enjoy practicing English with native speakers."	5.2	.82	3-6
32. "It is important to repeat and practice a lot in order to acquire good pronunciation."	5.6	.55	4-6

Note. Strongly Agree = 6 ; Agree = 5 ; Slightly Agree = 4 ; Slightly Disagree = 3 ; Disagree = 2; Strongly Disagree = 1.

Source: Author

    The last construct in the scale assessed learners' cultural affiliation with the L1 and L2. Means, ranges and standard deviations for items under the construct of cultural beliefs are fully reported in Table 4.11.

Table 4.11 Descriptive Statistics for cultural beliefs

Item	M	SD	Range
34. "I am fond of TV programs, music, and movies from English speaking countries."	5.3	.74	3-6
35. "Studying English is important because it will enable me to better understand and appreciate the English/American way of life."	4.8	1.1	2-6
36. "I like English."	5.1	.91	3-6
37. "To me my mother tongue (Portuguese) is more important than English."	3.9	1.5	1-6
38. "I prefer American/British movies and music to Brazilian movies and music."	3.4	1.5	1-6
39. "I often imagine myself as someone who is able to speak English well."	4.1	1.6	1-6

Note. Strongly Agree = 6 ; Agree = 5 ; Slightly Agree = 4 ; Slightly Disagree = 3 ; Disagree = 2; Strongly Disagree = 1 for items 34, 35, 36, 38, and 39. Strongly Agree = 1 ; Agree = 2 ; Slightly Agree = 3 ; Slightly Disagree = 4 ; Disagree = 5 ; Strongly Disagree = 6 for item 37.

Source: Author

On the whole, respondents manifested a positive orientation towards the L2 as well as a strong sense of affiliation towards the target language culture. However, cultural beliefs were not predictors of success in the phonological component of the L2, $r = .02$, $p = .90$.

4.6 *Self-assessment and language background variables*

In spite of self-confidence beliefs having achieved significance in predicting pronunciation accuracy, no relationship was found between learners' self-perceived and actual pronunciation performance. Most subjects failed to rate their own degree of foreign accentedness accurately, with the majority rating their pronunciation as a 5, 'noticeable foreign accent'. As expected, learners with the lowest scores on the pronunciation test tended to be the most lenient when rating their own phonological skills (see Fig. 4.1). These results are consonant with studies on self-assessments as they have consistently demonstrated that higher judges' scores tend to yield lower self-ratings, while overly confident learners generally receive the lowest scores on L2 performance (in Dlaska & Krekeler, 2008). This finding supports the Dunning-Kruger effect (in Dunning, 2011, p. 247), i.e.,

> poor performers in many social and intellectual domains seem largely unaware of just how deficient their expertise is. Their deficits leave them with a double burden—not only does their incomplete and misguided knowledge lead them to make mistakes but those exact same deficits also prevent them from recognizing when they are making mistakes and other people choosing more wisely.

I hypothesize that the inconsistency between successful learners' self-assessments and their self-confidence beliefs is related to individual factors which may be at play in performance self-ratings. Modesty may prevent certain learners from assigning high scores to their own phonological skills. Similarly, some speakers may be more critical towards their own performances than others. Some learners may have also been more comfortable to demonstrate their confidence with their own interlanguage phonology when answering questionnaire items. Likert-type questionnaire completion is, after all, a much less invasive method than learners' self-ratings.

We can infer from these findings that the relationship between mean ratings and learners' self-assessments differs across individuals. Thus, the results call for further self-assessment research in order to establish if this variable constitutes a reliable measure of actual performance.

Figure 4.1 Self-assessment and mean rating.

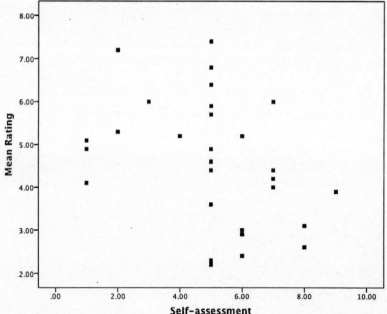

Source: Author

Furthermore, correlations were tabulated for outcome and language background variables. Length of residence in the UK, gender, and amount of continued L1 use were not found to be predictors of pronunciation accuracy, r = .29, p = .11, r = -.07, p = .67, and r = .02, p = .90, respectively. Conversely, the analysis revealed a significant relationship between age of first exposure to the target language and mean ratings. As seen in Table 4.12, learners who started learning English at a younger age were more likely to achieve higher scores on the pronunciation test. This finding lends support to studies on phonological attainment in which age of onset is consistently associated with pronunciation accuracy (see for example Moyer, 1999; Piske *et al.*, 2002 and Pullen, 2012).

Table 4.12. Subjects' age of onset: bivariate correlations.

Accent ratings	r	p	Sig. (2-tailed)
Task 1	-.42	.020	.05
Task 2	-.63	.001	.01
Task 3	-.57	.001	.01
Mean	-.59	.001	.01

4.7 *Summary of results*

Correlations between questionnaire constructs and pronunciation mean ratings revealed that beliefs about pronunciation acquisition and instruction, functional beliefs, pronunciation learning goals, learner strategies, and cultural beliefs were not predictors of pronunciation accuracy. Conversely, the constructs of emotional and self-confidence beliefs demonstrated significance for mean rating results, r= -.49, p < .01 and r= .42, p < .05, respectively.

The most statistically significant correlations (p < .01) appear between the item "I am happy with my present pronunciation" (r = .64) and the construct of emotional beliefs, particularly among the statements "I feel at ease when I have to speak English" (r = .57) and "I feel insecure about my pronunciation" (r = -.58). In addition, age of first exposure to the target language was a predictor of pronunciation performance (r = -.59). Slightly less powerful correlations (p < .05) were found between the construct of self-confidence beliefs and the items "I would take a pronunciation course if it were available to me" (r = -.42) and "my English pronunciation is below the average" (r=-.45).

Chapter Five

THE ROLE OF SOCIO-AFFECTIVE FACTORS ON L2 PRONUNCIATION ATTAINMENT

In this chapter I assess how the results from the investigation confirm or reject the hypotheses. I also analyze research findings in relation to the existing literature on the areas of L2 socio-psychological influences and pronunciation research.

5.1 *Emotional beliefs*

Together with learners' feelings of embarrassment and self-concept, the construct of emotional beliefs was devised with reference to studies on foreign language anxiety. Following Horwitz's (1986) Foreign Language Classroom Anxiety Scale (FLCAS) and Baran Łucarz's (2014) conceptualization of pronunciation anxiety, items on emotional beliefs were in fact specially included to measure learners' self-reported levels of pronunciation anxiety. Thus, we can conclude that the moderate negative relationship between the construct of emotional beliefs and subjects' pronunciation performance ($r = -.49$, $p < .01$) provides us with evidence that, along with low levels of embarrassment and inhibition, self-reported low pronunciation anxiety appears to be a predictor of L2 pronunciation accuracy.

In relation to previous findings on language anxiety (LA) and achievement, Matsuda and Gobel (2004) observe that although substantial research has revealed a negative relationship between LA and performance, the effects of facilitative anxiety (see section 2.2) have also been reported in the literature. Matsuda and Gobel contend that for this reason the results of foreign LA studies need to be treated with caution. Conversely, in a review of studies with a number of target languages and instructional contexts, Horwitz (2011) provides evidence that low levels of LA are indeed significant predictors of success in a foreign language. Despite the controversy surrounding the field, the findings from the present study support previous evidence for a negative correlation between language anxiety and attainment (see for example Horwitz, 2011 and Baran-Łucarz, 2012).

As previously mentioned, the construct of emotional beliefs also included emotions such as embarrassment and inhibition. With regard to these other variables, few studies to date have attempted to correlate them with pronunciation accuracy. Therefore, the finding that emotional beliefs affect pronunciation performance warrants further research.

Furthermore, the items "my pronunciation improves when I speak with non-native speakers" and "I feel less anxious when I speak with non-native speakers of English" follow research on the influence of the interlocutor on speakers' L2 oral performance (see for example Takahashi, 1989). Simply put, these items address the notion that L2 users react differently to non-native listeners than they do to their counterparts. It was hypothesized that L2 learners who feel anxious in NNS-NS interactions would obtain lower pronunciation scores. The correlation analysis revealed a moderate negative relationship between pronunciation performance and the item "my pronunciation improves when I speak with non-native speakers", $r = -.47$, $p < .01$, thus suggesting that higher levels of anxiety in interactions with native speakers of the target language appear to be detrimental to L2 pronunciation accuracy. Clearly, these results indicate the existence of a tight relationship between emotional beliefs and L2 phonological attainment.

5.2 *Self-confidence beliefs*

In the literature on language learning, self-confidence has been generally linked to self-efficacy and to the broader concept of self-esteem. While the latter consists of a global, trait-like variable, the former refers to "beliefs in one's capabilities to carry out certain specific tasks" (Dörnyei, 2005, p. 213). Brown (1980) refers to three levels of self-esteem: global, situation, and task. The first level is conceptualized in the literature as self-esteem per se, while the third pertains to the more specific variable of self-efficacy. The dimension identified in this study relates most closely to the second level, that is, to learners' overall assessment of their abilities in the target language since it investigates individuals' self-confidence in the particular context of second language acquisition.

Undeniably, learners' views about their performance in the target language become a crucial aspect of the ways in which they approach the task of learning a foreign language. Self-confidence has been indeed a wellestablished research tradition in applied linguistics (Dörnyei, 2005). In the present study, statistical analysis revealed a moderate positive relationship between the construct of self-confidence beliefs and outcome, $r = .42$, $p < .05$. These results support Gardner et al.'s (1997) investigation of ID variables and their relation to outcome. In their study, low anxiety ratings and self-confidence beliefs were found to be the strongest predictors of foreign language proficiency (see also Matsuda & Gobel, 2004).

Not only do the results from this volume indicate that self-confidence beliefs appear to have a bearing on pronunciation achievement, but the findings also indicate a relationship between overall self-perceived pronunciation competence and a specific self-belief, that is, satisfaction with one's own accent, e.g. "I am happy with my present English pronunciation" ($r = .64$, $p < .01$); "my English pronunciation is below the average" ($r = -.45$, $p < .05$). In Sifakis and Sougari (2005) a correlation was found between L2 teachers' satisfaction with their own accent and their amount of L2 use. In other words, instructors who were actively engaged in language use appeared to be happy with their accents. In addition to Sifakis and Sougaris' finding, the results from this undertaking implicate the need for research that isolates specific self-beliefs in studies of the interaction among self-confidence and language behaviors. Likewise, these results should be followed by investigations of specific self-beliefs and their relations to outcome.

Additionally, a moderate negative correlation ($r = -.42$, $p < .05$) was revealed between them item "I would take a pronunciation course if it were available to me" and mean ratings. Despite originally belonging to the construct of beliefs about pronunciation instruction, this statement seems to relate to subjects' self-confidence beliefs, and in particular with the self-belief of 'satisfaction with one's own accent'. Participants who are satisfied with their present pronunciation, after all, would not take efforts to improve their L2 phonological skills.

Contrary to most self-confidence studies, Tse (2000) found in her qualitative investigation of learners' beliefs about foreign language learning that students who received good grades in their coursework felt that they had not achieved a desired level of proficiency. Research with a mixed-methods approach may contribute to a better understanding of the correlations reported in the literature and may also shed light on the nature of learners' self-beliefs, how they are developed, and how emotions affect students' self-confidence.

In sum, the results of this study indicate the importance of learners' self-beliefs for pronunciation attainment and it strengthens previous findings on the existence of a relationship between positive self-beliefs and foreign language proficiency.

5.3 *The effects of affective variables on pronunciation attainment*

The construct of emotional beliefs in this study is closely linked to feelings of self-confidence and embarrassment, e.g. "I feel at ease when I have to speak English" ($r = .57$, $p < .01$); "I feel insecure about my English pronunciation" ($r = -.58$, $p < .01$). According to Aragão (2011), beliefs and emotions in SLA are interrelated and this relationship can be observed in the way students disclose beliefs about themselves as L2 learners. He theorizes that emotions such as embarrassment and self-esteem are influenced by beliefs associated with students' self-concepts and that these beliefs and emotions play a crucial role on the way learners see themselves as L2 users.

Indeed, a number of studies have demonstrated a tight interplay between the variables of self-confidence and emotional beliefs. Smit (2002), for example, found that self-efficacy beliefs and feelings of anxiety were important aspects of leaners' motivation in pronunciation learning. In Matsuda and Gobel (2001 in Matsuda & Gobel, 2004) low self-confidence was found to be a significant predictor of language anxiety. Supporting these findings, Gardner et al. (1997) report high correlations for the measure of language anxiety and self-confidence.

With regard to L2 pronunciation, self-beliefs and anxiety appear to be even more intertwined. The variable of pronunciation anxiety, for example, is strictly associated with pronunciation self-image, pronunciation self-assessment, fear of negative evaluation, and beliefs which are related to the importance attributed to L2 pronunciation (Baran-Łucarz, 2014). Several researchers in the field propose that affective[4] and personality factors seem to be the most powerful predictors of success in FL pronunciation (in Baran--Łucarz, 2012). By way of illustration, in Elliot (1995) learners' attitudes towards pronunciation were found to be the variable which related most to pronunciation accuracy.

The results of the present study strengthen these findings by revealing the interdependence of both variables. Unlike the other constructs within the taxonomy of pronunciation beliefs, moderate correlations were found between these two constructs and learners' pronunciation achievement. These results appear to suggest that affective variables exert an effect on L2 pronunciation attainment and may be more important to phonological performance than factors such as beliefs about pronunciation acquisition and instruction, pronunciation learning goals, pronunciation learning strategies or cultural beliefs.

5.4 *Demographic factors: age of onset*

Learners' pronunciation self-ratings and factual information, namely, gender, age of onset, length of residence, and amount of L2

---

[4] Affect is an umbrella term in SLA research, comprising aspects of emotion, feeling, judgment or attitude, which can condition behavior and influence language learning (Aragão, 2011).

use, were correlated for possible confounding factors. Significant correlations were only found for participants' age of first exposure to the target language (r = -.59, p < .01). Thus, in addition to self-confidence and emotional beliefs, age of onset (AO) seems to be a predictor of pronunciation competence. This finding fully corroborates research on L2 phonological attainment seeing that AO is the most commonly accepted predictor of pronunciation ability in the literature (see for example Moyer, 1999; Piske *et al.*, 2001; Pullen, 2012).

With regard to the variables of gender, length of residence, and amount of L2 use, research has been inconclusive in providing evidence of a stable relationship between these factors and language outcomes. Purcell and Suter (1980), Elliott (1995) and Piske *et al.* (2001), for example, report that learners' gender did not yield a significant effect on phonological achievement. The results from this study are consonant with these previous undertakings, thus strengthening the notion that gender does not seem to be a reliable predictor of pronunciation accuracy.

In this study, years of immersion in a target language environment varied widely but did not correlate with a higher mean rating for those subjects immersed longer, r = .29, p > .05. Therefore, a longer exposure in the target community did not lead to any greater phonological accuracy or consistency in ratings. This finding supports similar conclusions in previous studies for length of residence being a poor predictor of higher pronunciation accuracy (see for example Moyer, 1999 and Piske *et al.*, 2002).

Similarly, no significant correlations were found between amount of continued L2 use and outcome, r = .02, p = .90. Despite being a less important predictor of L2 pronunciation competence than AO, research on language use variables has demonstrated that frequent L1 use seems to be detrimental to pronunciation accuracy (see for example Flege *et al.*, 1997; Piske *et al.* 2001). Therefore, the finding from this undertaking does not corroborate previous evidence for a relation between amount of L1 or L2 use and pronunciation performance.

Furthermore, research on the relationship between outcome and learners' pronunciation self-ratings has provided ambiguous results. In Smit (2002) students' self-evaluation of their own accents proved to be the factor with the strongest impact on their pronunciation competence. Moyer (1999), however, found opposing results. Although Dlaska and Krekeler's (2008) findings support the conclusions drawn in Smit (2002), their analysis also revealed that learners rated their own sounds more strictly than the raters did. In the present volume, self-evaluation of phonological accuracy added no significant explanation to outcome and it therefore confirms the discrepancies between learners' self-perceived and externally evaluated pronunciation attainments reported in Moyer (1999) and Dlaska and Krekeler (2008). However, as reported in Figure 1 (see page 48), among the learners who did not rate their pronunciation achievement in the target language as a 'noticeable foreign accent', i.e., a score of 5/9 – which may indicate a ceiling effect -, many of the raters who received the lowest scores were also the most lenient, thus supporting the Dunning-Kruger effect (see page 47).

In relation to age of first exposure, as we have seen, this study supports the view that the earlier in life the target language is acquired, the better it will be pronounced. Thus, it appears to be in accordance with the Critical Period Hypothesis (see section 2.1). Nevertheless, future research with larger samples and distinct populations is needed to determine more precisely which conditions may induce successful mastery of the non-native phonological system.

Chapter Six

CONCLUSIONS

This chapter will provide an overall assessment of the results from the investigation. Next, the limitations of the study will be listed and its implications for L2 instruction will be presented. I conclude with suggestions for future research.

6.1 *Summary of research findings*

Several hypotheses formed the basis for the conception and implementation of this study. First, it was predicted that subjects with higher levels of pronunciation ability would share a set of beliefs related to L2 pronunciation. After statistical correlations were analyzed, self-confidence and emotional beliefs were the only variables found to exert a significant effect on mean ratings, while beliefs about pronunciation acquisition and instruction, functional beliefs, pronunciation learning goals, learning strategies, and cultural beliefs did not affect pronunciation outcomes.

Second, it was predicted that pronunciation beliefs associated with success in this skill would be in accordance with research on L2 phonological attainment. The results confirm this hypothesis as researchers in the field propose that affective and personality factors appear to be powerful predictors of success in L2 pronunciation (in Baran-Łucarz, 2012).

Finally, it was envisaged that beliefs about pronunciation may not operate independently as a predictor of phonological performance, being confounded with language background factors that contribute to the explanation of outcome. The interdependent variables were predicted to be gender, age of onset, length of residence, and amount of L2 use. Age of first exposure to the target language was the only factor which exerted an effect on outcome. This finding supports research on L2 phonological attainment since age of onset is the most commonly accepted predictor of pronunciation performance in the literature (see for example Moyer, 1999; Piske *et al.*, 2001; Pullen, 2012).

6.2 Limitations of the study

Certain limitations which are inherent in a study of this nature prevent us from interpreting the conclusions from this undertaking as ultimate answers to the acquisition of L2 pronunciation. The principal limitations concern its participant sampling procedures and instrumentation. Given the research methodology, the small sample size is certainly a caveat to this research. Time constraints did not permit data collection with a more representative sample and more research with larger sample sizes is thus needed to confirm the findings presented here.

The major limitation of this study, however, lies in the low reliability of the questionnaire, which may have had an effect on the statistical analyses. The reliability coefficient of the instrument used in this study had a value of .64. Skehan (1989) recommends researchers to aim at instruments with reliability coefficients in excess of .70. Although the items on the scale were carefully worded, piloted, and revised to ensure intelligibility, the variance may be attributable to the lack of interreliability of constructs within the scale.

Additionally, quantitative endeavors have limitations which restrict the interpretability and generalizability of their results. We cannot decisively conclude that associations between the variables are inexistent when the analysis fails to detect them. A true association may be statistically insignificant due to the experiment's design. As previously mentioned, in this study not enough participants were included to observe findings in sufficient numbers. Therefore, we cannot dismiss the non-significant variables as irrelevant. Mixed-methods studies are also needed to determine more precisely which pronunciation beliefs are conducive to outcome.

The use of questionnaires may have also affected the results. Employing questionnaires in studies about learners' views prevents participants from providing in-depth analysis of each response. What is more, questionnaire implementation restricts learners' answers seeing that their responses need to be based on a pre-established set of statements (Barcelos, 2003). For these reasons, Victori (1999 in Barcelos, 2003) recommends the application of semi-open ended instruments and triangulation of methods in beliefs about SLA research. The research framework adopted for this study as well as time constraints did not permit qualitative inquiry. A mixed-methods approach appears to be more appropriate for research on the effects of socio-psychological factors on language outcome.

In what regards the rating-judgment study, despite sharing that they had little to no previous experience with Brazilian ESL accented speech, judges' responses may have been influenced by factors which include their preferences to particular voices (Derwing and Munro, 2005). In addition, subjects' level of stress when performing the tasks may have had an effect on their performance (in Elliot, 2003).

6.3 *Pedagogical and theoretical implications*

Notwithstanding its limitations, the results from this study, if corroborated by further research, could have important implications for language pedagogy. The fundamental reason for conducting empirical studies of this nature is, after all, the language classroom. The findings indicate that reducing learners' anxiety and enhancing their self-confidence should become primary objectives in the pronunciation classroom. Language educators can achieve this by creating a comfortable learning atmosphere, encouraging their students' involvement in classroom activities, providing guidance, and fostering learners' autonomy. This study also reveals the need for the design of methodological strategies aimed at helping learners develop confidence in the target language.

An important next step would be a mixed-methods description of the concrete nature of learners' beliefs about L2 pronunciation.

Other areas for future research include more rigorous studies which set to unravel the effects of pronunciation beliefs on language achievement, studies which assess methodologies aimed at changing detrimental beliefs about SLA, and research which examines the relationship between learner beliefs and other foreign language skills. In addition, the results suggest the need for more studies on the effects of emotions and self-beliefs on language outcomes. The relation between these variables and other language skills should also be investigated. Finally, the field of SLA would certainly benefit from the design of future taxonomies of pronunciation beliefs. In sum, this research contributes to a primary understanding of the ways in which beliefs about pronunciation may affect learners' phonological competence in the target language. Findings from future research will prove to be particularly fruitful in helping us integrate practices which are conducive to pronunciation attainment into the second language classroom. Our ultimate goal as language educators should be to provide instruction which is effective in improving all aspects of foreign language acquisition, and research such as this serves as a step towards achieving this goal.

REFERENCES

Aragão, R. (2011). Beliefs and emotions in foreign language learning. *System, 39*, 302-313.

Azevedo, M. (1981). *Contrastive phonology of Portuguese and English.* Washington: Georgetown University Press.

Baptista, B. (2000). The learning and teaching of pronunciation in Brazil: linking research and practice. *Speak Out!, 25,* 12-19.

Baran-Łucarz, M. (2007). Profiles of excellent, very good, and very poor foreign language pronunciation learners. *Speak Out!, 38,* 5-10.

Baran-Łucarz, M. (2011). The relationship between language anxiety and the actual and perceived levels of FL pronunciation. *Studies in Second Language Learning and Teaching, 1*(4), 491-514.

Baran-Łucarz, M. (2012). Ego boundaries and attainments in FL pronunciation. *Studies in Second Language Learning and Teaching, 2*(1), 45-66.

Baran-Łucarz, M. (May. 2014). *"Pronunciation anxiety and WTC in a FL outside the classroom."* Matters of the Mind: Psychology and Language Learning: Graz, Austria. University of Graz, Austria.

Baratieri, J. (2006). *Production of /l/ in the English coda by Brazilian EFL learners: an acoustic-articulatory analysis.* (Master dissertation). Universidade Federal de Santa Catarina.

Barcelos, A. M. F. (2003) Researching Beliefs about SLA: A Critical Review. In P.Kalaja, & A. M. F, Barcelos (Eds.), *Beliefs about SLA: New Research Approaches.* (pp. 7-33). New York: Springer.

Barcelos, A. M. F. (May. 2014). *"The ecology of language learning beliefs, emotions, and identities."* Matters of the Mind: Psychology and Language Learning: Graz, Austria. University of Graz, Austria.

Bernat, E. & Gvozdenko, I. (2005). Beliefs about Language Learning: Current Knowledge, Pedagogical Implications, and New Research Directions.

Teaching English as a Second or Foreign Language, 9(1). Online. Available at http://www.tesl-ej.org/ej33/a1.html.

Bettoni-Techio, M. & Koerich, R. (2006). Palatalization in Brazilian Portuguese/ English interphonology. *Revista Virtual de Estudos da Linguagem-ReVEL, 4*(7), 1-17.

Bettoni-Techio, M. & Koerich, R. (2008). Preceding phonological context effects on palatalization in Brazilian Portuguese/ English interphonology. *Ilha do Desterro, 55,* 63-81.

Bongaerts, T., Planken, B., & Schils, E. (1995). Can late starters attain a native accent in a foreign language? A test of the Critical Period Hypothesis. In D. Singleton & Z. Lengyel (Eds.), *The age factor in second language acquisition: a critical look at the Critical Period Hypothesis.* Clevedon: Multilingual Matters.

Bongaerts, T. (1999). Ultimate attainment in L2 pronunciation: the case of very advanced late L2 learners. In D. Birdsong (Ed.), *Second Language Acquisition and the Critical Period Hypothesis.* (pp. 133-155). New Jersey: Lawrence Erlbaum Associates.

Brawerman-Albini, A. & Becker, M. (2014). Perception and production of English stress by Brazilian speakers. Proceedings of the International Symposium on the Acquisition of Second Language Speech Concordia Working Papers in Applied Linguistics, COPAL, 5, 73-84.

Burri, M. (2023). "Comparing L2 Teachers' Practices With Learners' Perceptions of English Pronunciation Teaching." *Profile: Issues in Teachers' Professional Development, 25*(1), 129-145.

Breitkreutz, J., Derwing, T., & Rossiter, M. (2001). Pronunciation Teaching Practices in Canada. *TESL Canada Journal, 19,* 51-61.

Brown, H. D. (1980). *Principles of Language Learning and Teaching.* Englewood Cliffs, N. J.: Prentice Hall.

Brown, A. (2008). Pronunciation and good language learners In C. Griffiths (Ed.), *Lessons from good language learners.* (pp. 197-207). Cambridge: Cambridge University Press.

Brown, A. (2009). Students' and teachers' perceptions of effective foreign language teaching: a comparison of ideals. *The Modern Language Journal, 93*(1), 46-60.

Brown, J. (2001). *Using surveys in language programs.* Cambridge: Cambridge University Press.

Burgess, J. & Spencer, S. (2000). Phonology and Pronunciation in Integrated Language Teaching and Teacher Education. *System, 28*(2), 191-215.

Calka, A. (2011). Pronunciation learning strategies-identification and classification. In M. Pawlak, E. Waniek-Klimczak & J. Majer (Eds.), *Speaking and instructed foreign language acquisition.* (pp. 149-168). Bristol: Multilingual Matters.

Cardoso, W. (2007). The variable development of English word--final stops by Brazilian Portuguese speakers: a stochastic optimally theoretic account. *Language Variation and Change, 19,* 1-30.

Cenoz, J. & Lecumberri, M. (1999). The Acquisition of English Pronunciation: Learners' Views. *International Journal of Applied Linguistics, 9*(1), 3-17.

Cotterall, S. (1995). Readiness for autonomy: investigating learner beliefs. *System, 23*(2), 195-205.

Dalton-Puffer, C.; Kaltenboeck, G., & Smit, U. (1997). Learner attitudes and L2 pronunciation in Austria. *World Englishes, 16*(1), 115-128.

Dalton, C. & Smit, U. (1997). On the motivation of advanced pronunciation learners. *Speak Out!, 21,* 5-9.

Deneckere, M. (2011). Learners' beliefs and affect in early English pronunciation learning: a study on instructed and non-instructed children's attitudes towards English pronunciation learning in Flanders. (Master's dissertation). Ghent University.

Derwing, T. (2008). Curriculum issues in teaching pronunciation to second language learners. In J. Ewards & M. Zampini (Eds.), *Phonology and Second Language Acquisition.* (pp. 347-369). Amsterdam: John Benjamins.

Derwing, T. & Munro, M. (1997). Accent, intelligibility, and comprehensibility: evidence from four L1s. *Studies in Second Language Acquisition, 19*(1), 1-16.

Derwing, T. & Munro, M. (2005). Second Language Accent and Pronunciation Teaching: A Research-Based Approach. *TESOL Quarterly, 39*(3), 379-395.

Derwing, T. & Rossiter, M. (2002). ESL Learners' Perceptions of Their Pronunciation Needs and Strategies. *System, 30*, 155-166.

Derwing, T. M., Thomson, R. I., & Munro, M. J. (2006). English pronunciation and fluency development in Mandarin and Slavic speakers. *System, 34*, 183-193.

Dlaska, A. & Krekeler, C. (2008). Self-assessment of pronunciation. *System, 36*, 506-516.

Dörnyei, Z. (2005). Other learner characteristics. In Dörnyei, Z. *The Psychology of the language learner: individual differences in Second Language Acquisition.* (pp. 197-217). London: Lawrence Erlbaum.

Dörnyei, Z. (2013). The relationship between language aptitude and language learning motivation: individual differences from a dynamic systems perspective. In E. Macaro (Ed.), *The Bloomsbury companion to second language acquisition.* (pp. 247-267). London: Bloomsbury Companions.

Dunning, D. (2011). The Dunning–Kruger effect: On being ignorant of one's own ignorance. *Advances in experimental social psychology*, (44), 247-296.

Eisenstein, M. & Starbuck, R. (1989). The effect of emotional investment on L2 production. In S. Gass, C. Madden, D. Preston, & L. Selinker (Eds.), *Variation in second language acquisition volume II: psycholinguistic issues.* (pp. 125-137). Clevedon: Multilingual Matters.

El-Dash, L. & Busnardo, J. (2001). Brazilian attitudes toward English: dimensions of status and solidarity. *International Journal of Applied Linguistics, 11*(1), 57-74.

Elliott, R. (2003). Staking out the territory at the turn of the century: integrating phonological theory, research, and the effect of formal instruction on pronunciation in the acquisition of Spanish as a Second Language. In B. Lafford & R. Salaberry (Eds.), *Spanish Second Language Acquisition: state of the science.* (pp. 19-46). Georgetown: Georgetown University Press.

Fang, Z. (1996). A review of research on teacher beliefs and practices. *Educational Research, 38*(1), 47-65.

Fisher, L. (May. 2014). *"Constructing learner beliefs in the languages classroom using metaphor."* Matters of the Mind: Psychology and Language Learning: Graz, Austria. University of Graz, Austria.

Flege, J., Frieda, E., & Nozawa, T. (1997). Amount of native-language (L1) use affects the pronunciation of an L2. *Journal of Phonetics, 25*(2), 169-186.

Gabillon, Z. (2007). Learner beliefs on L2 attitudes and motivation: An exploratory study. *Lingua et Linguistica, 1*(1), 68-90.

Gardner, R. (1979). Social Psychological Aspects of Second Language Acquisition. In H. Giles, & R. Stclair (Eds.), *Language and Social Psychology.* (pp. 193-220). Oxford: Basil Blackwell.

Gatbonton, E., Trofimovich, P., & Magid, M. (2005). Learners' ethnic group affiliation and L2 pronunciation accuracy: a sociolinguistic investigation. *TESOL Quarterly, 39*(3), 489-509.

Gardner, R., Tremblay, P., & Masgoret, A. M. (1997). Towards a Full Model of Second Language Learning: An Empirical Investigation. *The Modern Language Journal, 81*(3), 344-362.

Goh, C. & Chen, Z. (2014). Teaching spoken English in China: the relationship between beliefs and characteristics of university EFL teachers. In: S. Said & L. Zhang (Eds.), *Language teachers and teaching: global perspectives, local initiatives.* (pp. 109-125). London: Routledge.

Golovatch, Y. & Vanderplank, R. (2007). Unwitting agents: the role of adult learners' attributions of success in shaping language--learning behaviour. *Journal of Adult and Continuing Education, 13*(2), 127-155. Gregersen & MacIntyre, 2014

Gregersen, T. & MacIntyre, P. (2014). *Capitalizing on Language Learners' Individuality: from premise to practice*. Bristol: Multilingual Matters.

Griffiths, C. (Ed.). (2008). *Lessons from good language learners*. Cambridge: Cambridge University Press. Hammond, R. (1995) Foreign accent and phonetic interference: the application of linguistic research to the teaching of second language pronunciation. In F. Eckman, D. Highland, P. Lee, J. Mileham, & R. Weber (Eds.), *Second language acquisition theory and pedagogy*. (pp. 293-303). Mahwah, NJ: Lawrence Erlbaum Associates.

Holec, H. (1987). The Learner as Manager: Managing Learning or Managing to Learn? In A. Wenden & J. Rubin (Eds.), *Learner Strategies in Language Learning*. (pp. 145-157). Hertforshire: Prentice Hall International.

Horwitz, E. (1985). Using student beliefs about language learning and teaching in the foreign language methods course. *Foreign Language Annals, 18*(4), 333-340.

Horwitz, E. K., Horwitz, M. B., & Cope, J. (1986). Foreign language classroom anxiety. *The Modern Language Journal, 70*(2), 125-132.

Horwitz, E. (1987). Surveying student beliefs about language learning. In A. Wenden & J. Rubin (Eds.), *Learner Strategies in Language Learning*. (pp. 119-132). Hertforshire:

Prentice Hall International.

Horwitz, E. (1988). The beliefs about language learning of beginning foreign language students. *Modern Language Journal, 72*(3), 283-294.

Horwitz, E. (1999). Cultural and situational influences on foreign language learners' beliefs about language learning: a review of BALLI studies. *System, 27*(4), 557-576.

Horwitz, E. (2001). Language anxiety and achievement. *Annual Review of Applied Linguistics, 21*, 112-126.

Hua, Congchao. (2023). "Pronunciation assessment of learners, by learners, and for learners: Effects, validity and reliability, and learners' perception." *Language Teaching Research, 0*(0).

Ioup, G. (1989) Immigrant children who have failed to acquire native English. In S. Gass, C. Madden, D. Preston, & L. Selinker (Eds.), *Variation in second language acquisition, volume 2: psycholinguistic issues.* (pp. 160-173). Clevedon: Multilingual Matters.

Isaacs, T. & Harding, L. (2017). Pronunciation assessment. *Language Teaching, 50*(3), 347-366.

Isaacs, T. (2009). Integrating form and meaning in L2 pronunciation instruction. *TESL Canada Journal, 27*(1), 1-11.

Isaacs, T. & Thomson, R. (2013). Rater experience, rating scale length, and judgments of L2 pronunciation: revisiting research conventions. *Language Assessment Quarterly, 10*, 135-159.

Jenkins, J. (2004). Research in teaching pronunciation and intonation. *Annual Review of Applied Linguistics, 24*, 109-125.

Jesney, K. (2004). *The use of global foreign accent rating in studies of L2 acquisition.* Calgary, AB: University of Calgary Language Research Centre Reports. Online. Available at http://www--bcf.usc.edu/~jesney/Jesney2004GlobalAccent.pdf.

Jilka, M. (2009a). Talent and proficiency in language. In G. Dogil & S. Reiterer (Eds.), *Language talent and brain activity.* (pp. 1-16). New York: Mouton de Gruyter.

Jilka, M. (2009b). Assessment of phonetic ability. In G. Dogil & S. Reiterer (Eds.), *Language talent and brain activity.* (pp. 17-66). New York: Mouton de Gruyter.

Jones, R. (1997). Beyond "Listen and Repeat": Pronunciation Teaching Materials and Theories of Second Language Acquisition. *System, 25*(1), 103-112.

Jun, H. G. & Li, J. (2010). Factors in raters' perceptions of comprehensibility and accentedness. In J. Levis & K. LeVelle (Eds.), *Proceedings of the 1st Pronunciation in Second Language Learning and Teaching Conference,* Iowa State University, Sept. 2009. (pp. 53-66). Ames, IA: Iowa State University.

Kalaja, P. & Barcelos, A. M. F. (Eds.). (2003). *Beliefs about SLA: New Research Approaches.* New York: Springer.

Kang, O. (2010). ESL learners' attitudes toward pronunciation instruction and varieties of English. In J. Levis & K. LeVelle (Eds.), *Proceedings of the 1st Pronunciation in Second Language Learning and Teaching Conference,* Iowa State University, Sept. 2009. (pp. 105-118). Ames, IA: Iowa State University.

Kaypak, E. & Ortaçtepe, D. (2014). Language learner beliefs and study abroad: a study on English as a lingua franca (ELF). *System, 42,* 355-367.

Kluge, D. (2004). *Perception and production of English syllable--final nasals by Brazilian learners.* (Master's thesis). Online. Available at https://repositorio.ufsc.br/bitstream/handle/123456789/87658/212390.pdf?s equence=1s.

Keys, K. (2002). First language influence on the spoken English of Brazilian students of EFL. *ELT Journal, 56*(1), 41-46.

Ladegaard, H. & Sachdev, I. (2006). 'I like the Americans...but I certainly don't aim for an American accent': language attitudes, vitality and foreign language learning in Denmark. *Journal of Multilingual and Multicultural Development, 27*(2), 91-108.

Léger, D. & Storch (2009). Learners' perceptions and attitudes: implications for willingness to communicate in an L2 classroom. *System, 37,* 269-285.

Lengyel, Z. (1995). Some critical remarks on the phonological component. In D. Singleton & Z. Lengyel (Eds.), *The age factor in Second Language Acquisition: a critical look at the Critical Period Hypothesis.* (pp. 124-134). Clevedon: Multilingual Matters.

Levis, J. (2005). Changing contexts and shifting paradigms in pronunciation teaching. *TESOL Quarterly, 39*(3), 369-377.

Levis, J. (1999). Intonation in Theory and Practice, Revisited. *TESOL Quarterly, 33*(1), 37-63.

Macaro, E. (2003). *Teaching and Learning a Second Language.* London: Continuum.

Macaro, E. (2013). *The Bloomsbury Companion to Second Language Acquisition.* London: Bloomsbury Companions.

Macken, M. & Ferguson, C. (1981). Phonological universals in language acquisition. In H. Winitz (Ed.), *Native and foreign language acquisition.* (pp. 110-129). New York: New York Academy of Sciences.

Major, R., Fitzmaurice, S., Bunta, F., Balasubramanian, C. (2002). The Effects of Nonnative Accents on Listening Comprehension: Implications for ESL Assessment. *TESOL Quarterly, 36*(2), 173-189.

Mantle-Bromley, C. (1995). Positive attitudes and realistic beliefs: links to proficiency. *The Modern Language Journal, 79*(3), 372-384.

Matsuda, S. & Gobel, P. (2004). Anxiety and predictors of performance in the foreign language classroom. *System, 32*, 21-36.

Meerleer, M. (2012). *Beliefs and attitudes towards English as a Lingua Franca: native and non--native pronunciation. A Flemish and Walloon perspective.* (Master dissertation) Ghent University.

Mills, R. (May. 2014). "Self--efficacy in second language acquisition." Matters of the Mind: Psychology and Language Learning: Graz, Austria. University of Graz, Austria.

Morley, J. (1991). The pronunciation component in teaching English to speakers of other languages. *TESOL Quarterly, 25*(3), 481-519.

Moyer, A. (2007). Do language attitudes determine accent? A study of Bilinguals in the USA. *Journal of Multilingual and Multicultural Development, 28*(6), 502-518.

Moyer, A. (1999). Ultimate attainment in L2 phonology: the critical factors of age, motivation, and instruction. *Studies in Second Language Acquisition, 21*(1), 81-108.

Müller, M. (2011). *Learners' identity negotiations and beliefs about pronunciation in study abroad contexts.* Ph.D. Thesis. University of Waterloo: Canada.

Munro, M. & Derwing, T. (1995). Processing time, accent, and comprehensibility in the perception of native and foreign-accented speech. *Language and Speech, 38*(3), 289-306.

Naiman, N., Fröhlich, M., Stern, H. H., & Todesco, A. (1978). *The Good Language Learner.* Clevedon: Multilingual Matters.

Norton, B. & Toohey, K. (2001). Changing Perspectives on Good Language Learners. *TESOL Quarterly, 35*(2), 307-322.

Nowacka, M. (2012). Questionnaire--Based Pronunciation Studies: Italian, Spanish and Polish Students' Views on Their English Pronunciation. *Research in Language, 10*(1), 43-61.

Nunnally, J. C. (1978). *Psychometric theory* (2nd ed.). New York: McGraw-Hill.

Obler, L. (1989). Exceptional second language learners. In S. Gass, C. Madden, C., D. Preston, & L. Selinker (Eds.), *Variation in Second Language Acquisition: volume*

II: psycholinguistic issues. (pp. 141-157). Clevedon: Multilingual Matters.

Osborne, D. (2008). Systematic differences in consonant sounds between the interlanguage phonology of a Brazilian learner of English and Standard American English. *Ilha do Desterro. A Journal of English Language, Literatures in English and*

Cultural Studies, 55, 111-132.

Otlowski, M. (1998). Pronunciation: what are the expectations? *The Internet TESL*

Journal, 4(1). Online. Available at http://iteslj.org/Articles/Otlowski--Pronunciation.

Peacock, M. (1999). Beliefs about language learning and their relationship to proficiency. *International Journal of Applied Linguistics, 9*(2), 247-265.

Perozzo, R. & Alves, U. (2014). Perception of English word--final unreleased consonants by Brazilian EFL learners. *Proceedings of the International*

Symposium on the Acquisition of Second Language Speech Concordia Working Papers in Applied Linguistics, COPAL, 5, 514-528.

Piller, I. (2002). Passing for a native speaker: Identity and success in second language learning. *Journal of Sociolinguistics,* 6(2), 179-206.

Piske, T., MacKay, I., & Flege, J. (2001). Factors affecting degree of foreign accent in an L2: a review. *Journal of Phonetics,* 29, 191-215.

Politzer, R. & McGroarty, M. (1985). An exploratory study of learning behaviors and their relationship to gains in linguistic and communicative competence. *TESOL Quarterly,* 19(1), 103-123.

Pullen, E. (2012). Cultural identity, pronunciation, and attitudes of Turkish speakers of English: language identity in an EFL context. In J. Levis & K. LeVelle (Eds.), *Proceedings of the 3rd Pronunciation in Second Language Learning and Teaching Conference, Sept. 2011.* (pp. 65-83). Ames, IA: Iowa State University.

Purcell, E. & Suter, R. (1980). Predictors of Pronunciation Accuracy: a Reexamination. *Language Learning,* 30(2), 271-287.

Reis, M. (2006). *The perception and production of English interdental fricatives by Brazilian EFL learners.* (Master dissertation). Universidade Federal de Santa Catarina.

Rieger, B. (2009). Gender and target language effect on beliefs about language learning. *Practice and Theory in Systems of Education,* 4(3-4), 101-114.

Rogerson-Revell, P. (2011). Research and L2 phonological acquisition. In *English phonology and pronunciation teaching.* (pp. 16-25). London: Continuum.

Rossiter, M. J. (2009). Perceptions of L2 fluency by native and non-native speakers of English. *Canadian Modern Language Review,* 65, 395-412.

Ryan, S. (2009). Self and identity in L2 motivation in Japan: the ideal L2 self and Japanese learners of English. In Z. Dörnyei & E. Ushioda (Ed.), *Motivation, language identity and the L2 self.* (pp. 120-143). Bristol: Multilingual Matters.

Saito, K. (2023). How does having a good ear promote successful second language speech acquisition in adulthood? Introducing Auditory Precision Hypothesis-L2. *Language Teaching,* 1-17.

Sardegna, V. G. (2012). Learner differences in strategy use, self--efficacy beliefs, and pronunciation improvement. In J. Levis & K. LeVelle (Eds.), *Proceedings of the 3rd Pronunciation in Second Language Learning and Teaching Conference, Sept. 2011.* (pp. 39-53). Ames, IA: Iowa State University.

Scales, J., Wennerstrom, A., Richard, D., & Wu, S. (2006). Language Learners' Perceptions of Accent. *TESOL Quarterly, 40*(4), 715-738.

Schaetzel, K. & Low, E. (2009). Teaching pronunciation to adult English language learners. *Caella Network,* 2-8.

Schumann, J. H. (1986). Research on the acculturation model of second language acquisition. *Journal of Multilingualism and Multicultural Development, 7*(5), 379-392.

Seliger, H. & Shohamy, E. (1989). The Preparatory Stages of Research. *Second Language Research Methods,* Oxford: OUP, 43-63.

Setter, J. & Jenkins, J. (2005). State-of-the-art review article: pronunciation. *Language Teaching, 38,* 1-17.

Sifakis, N. & Sougari, A. (2005) Pronunciation issues and EIL pedagogy in the periphery: a survey of Greek state school teachers' beliefs. *TESOL Quarterly, 39*(3), 467-487.

Silva, R. (1999). An investigation into the intelligibility of the pronunciation of Brazilian intermediate students. *Speak out!, 25,* 35-43.

Simon, E. (2005). How native-like do you want to sound? A study on the pronunciation target of advanced learners of English in Flanders. *Moderna Sprak, 99*(1), 12-21.

Simon, E. & Taveniers, M. (2011). Advanced EFL learners' beliefs about language learning and teaching: A comparison between grammar, pronunciation, and vocabulary. *English Studies, 92*(8), 896-922.

Skehan, P. (1989). Methodological considerations in ID research. In P. Skehan, *Individual differences in second language learning.* (pp. 10-24). London: Edward Arnold.

Smit, U. (2002). The interaction of motivation and achievement in advanced EFL pronunciation learners. *IRAL, 40,* 89-116.

Sobkowiak, W. (2002). English speech in Polish eyes: what university students think about English pronunciation teaching and learning. In: E. Waniek-Klimczar & P. Melia (Eds.), *Accents and speech in teaching English phonetics and phonology: EFL perspective.* (pp. 97-105). Frankfurt: Peter Lang.

Stanojevic, M., Borenic, V., Smojver, V. (2012). Combining Different Types of data in Studying Attitudes to English as a Lingua Franca. *Research in Language, 10*(1), 29-41.

Stefanova, D. & Shenkova, T. (2010). Theoretical aspects of studying beliefs about language learning (based on the piloting of a research questionnaire). Online. Available at http://conf.uni-ruse.bg/bg/docs/cp10/6.3/6.3-30.pdf.

Szyszka, M. (2011). Foreign language anxiety and self--perceived English pronunciation competence. *Studies in Second Language Learning and Teaching, 2,* 283-300.

Takahashi, T. (1989) The influence of the listener on L2 speech. In S. Gass, C. Madden, D. Preston, & L. Selinker (Eds.), *Variation in Second Language Acquisition: discourse and pragmatics.* (pp. 245-277). Clevedon: Multilingual Matters.

Tergujeff, E. (2013). Learner Perspective on English Pronunciation Teaching in an EFL Context. *Research in Language, 11*(1), 81-95.

Trofimovich, P. (2013). Interactive alignment: a teaching-friendly view of second language pronunciation learning. *Language Teaching,* 1-12.

Tse, L. (2000). Student perceptions of foreign language study: a qualitative analysis of foreign language autobiographies. *The Modern Language Journal, 84*(1), 69-82.

Van Schoor, D. (2010). *Learners' beliefs about pronunciation training in Flanders.* (Master dissertation). Ghent University.

Waniek-Klimczak, E. (2011). "I am good at speaking, but I failed my phonetics class"-- pronunciation and speaking in advanced learners of English. In M. Pawlak, E. Waniek-Klimczak, & J. Majer (Eds.), *Speaking and instructed foreign language acquisition.* (pp. 117-129). Bristol: Multilingual Matters.

White, C. (2008). Beliefs and good language learners. In C. Griffiths (Ed.), *Lessons from good language learners.* (pp. 121-130). Cambridge: Cambridge University Press.

Williams, M., Burden, R., Poulet, G., & Maun, I. (2004). Learners' perceptions of their successes and failures in foreign language learning. *Language Learning Journal, 30,* 19-29.

Yang, N. (1999). The Relationship Between EFL Learner's Beliefs and Learning Strategy Use. *System, 27,* 515-535.

Yu, C. (2013). Do learner beliefs about learning matter in English language education? *Malaysian Journal of ELT Research, 9*(2), 19-35.

APPENDICES

APPENDIX 1

Consent Form

My name is Lais de Oliveira Borges and I am a full-time MA researcher at the Institute of Education, University College London. I am currently investigating what beliefs about the acquisition and instruction of English pronunciation are associated with success in this skill among Brazilian learners in British educational settings. This study will contribute towards a better understanding of successful learners' perceptions about pronunciation acquisition, which can ultimately lead to the development of pedagogical strategies aimed at restructuring beliefs of poor language learners.

Please will you help me with my research? Here are some notes that you might want to think about before you decide:

A 4-page multiple-scale questionnaire that has a 20-min completion limit will be administered either in one-to-one or group administration formats. The questionnaire data will be collected anonymously. The contents of this form are absolutely confidential and information identifying the respondent will not be disclosed under any circumstances. After the questionnaire completion, your speech will be recorded and this procedure will take approximately 10 minutes. This procedure consists of two stages: a word list, sentences and paragraph read-aloud, followed by a free--response to one of three prompts provided by the researcher. Once again, the recordings will be kept private.

Participation in this project is voluntary and you are free to withdraw from it at any time. In no way does this waive your legal rights nor release the investigators, or involved institutions from their legal and professional responsibilities. The research will not help you, but you may decide it is worth taking part because the findings might help people in the future. If you would like to receive information about the findings of this study, a summary will be forwarded to you when the study is finished.

It is up to you to decide if you want to help us. If you do consent, you can still say 'pass' or 'stop' during an interview, and you can drop out of the project at any time.

The Institute of Education Research Ethics Board has approved this research study.

I have read the information leaflet and I agree to:

- Take part in a 5 min taped activity; ( )
- Allow my answers to be read. ( )

Date: _____
Name: _____
Signature: _____

Researcher:

I have discussed the project and answered any further questions.

Date: _____
Signature: _____

APPENDIX 2

Questionnaire – Portuguese Version

Questionário Sobre Crenças de Alunos Brasileiros em Relação à Pronúncia de Inglês Como Segunda Língua

No.:_____

Nós gostaríamos que você nos ajudasse respondendo às seguintes perguntas em relação ao aprendizado de língua estrangeira. Esta análise é conduzida pelo Institute of Education da University College London para melhor entender as crenças de alunos em relação à pronúncia de inglês como segunda língua. Isto não é um teste, portanto, não existem respostas "certas" ou "erradas". Nós estamos interessados na sua opinião pessoal. Muito obrigada pela sua ajuda.

Parte I

Nesta parte, nós gostaríamos que você nos informasse o quanto você concorda ou discorda com as seguintes declarações. Circule um número de 1 a 6. Por favor, não deixe nenhum item em branco.

Discordo Plenamente	Discordo	Discordo Ligeiramente	Concordo Ligeiramente	Concordo	Concordo Plenamente
1	2	3	4	5	6

Por exemplo, se você acha que esta declaração é verdadeira, mas é de alguma forma exagerada, você deve circular 4 ou 5.	
Chocolate não é saudável.	1 2 3 4 5 6

1. É mais fácil para crianças do que para adultos utilizar pronúncia correta em língua estrangeira.	1 2 3 4 5 6
2. Algumas pessoas nascem com uma habilidade especial que as ajudam a aprender e a utilizar pronúncia correta em língua estrangeira.	1 2 3 4 5 6
3. Sua proficiência na pronúncia de inglês depende de fatores sobre os quais você tem pouco controle.	1 2 3 4 5 6
4. É melhor aprender pronúncia em inglês em um país de língua inglesa.	1 2 3 4 5 6
5. O ensino de pronúncia deve ser incluído em aulas de inglês.	1 2 3 4 5 6
6. Eu me matricularia em um curso de pronúncia, se fosse disponível para mim.	1 2 3 4 5 6
7. O aprendizado de símbolos fonéticos (por exemplo, /æ/,/ʌ/,/əə/ etc.) em aulas de inglês pode melhorar minha pronúncia.	1 2 3 4 5 6
8. Eu acredito que a produção do meu/minha professor(a) me fornece um excelente modelo de pronúncia em língua inglesa.	1 2 3 4 5 6
9. Eu me sinto confortável quando tenho que falar em inglês.	1 2 3 4 5 6
10. Eu não me sinto confiante em relação à minha pronúncia.	1 2 3 4 5 6
11. Minha pronúncia melhora quando falo com falantes não nativos.	1 2 3 4 5 6
12. Eu me sinto menos ansioso quando falo com falantes não nativos de inglês.	1 2 3 4 5 6
13. Ter uma boa pronúncia em inglês é importante para minha carreira profissional.	1 2 3 4 5 6
14. Uma boa pronúncia em inglês vai me permitir me tornar um membro influente na minha comunidade.	1 2 3 4 5 6
15. Uma boa pronúncia em inglês vai me permitir interagir mais facilmente	1 2 3 4 5 6
com falantes nativos de inglês.	
16. Uma boa pronúncia em inglês vai me permitir interagir mais facilmente com pessoas que não falam a minha língua.	1 2 3 4 5 6

Parte II

Por favor, responda a estas novas perguntas da mesma forma que você fez anteriormente.

Discordo Plenamente	Discordo	Discordo Ligeiramente	Concordo Ligeiramente	Concordo	Concordo Plenamente
1	2	3	4	5	6

17. Eu acho que tenho aptidão em língua estrangeira (uma habilidade especial no aprendizado de línguas estrangeiras).	1 2 3 4 5 6
18. Eu acredito que um dia posso vir a falar inglês muito bem.	1 2 3 4 5 6
19. Estou satisfeito com minha presente pronúncia em inglês.	1 2 3 4 5 6
20. Minha pronúncia em inglês é abaixo da média.	1 2 3 4 5 6
21. Às vezes consigo passar por um falante nativo em interações curtas.	1 2 3 4 5 6
22. Eu tento imitar a pronúncia de falantes nativos de inglês.	1 2 3 4 5 6
23. É importante falar em inglês com uma excelente pronúncia.	1 2 3 4 5 6
24. Eu não gosto quando pessoas reconhecem no meu sotaque que eu não sou um falante nativo de inglês.	1 2 3 4 5 6
25. Eu quero falar em inglês com um sotaque que não esteja relacionado a nenhum país de língua inglesa.	1 2 3 4 5 6
26. Eu estou contente com minha pronúncia, contanto que as pessoas consigam me entender.	1 2 3 4 5 6
27. Eu não me importo que as pessoas consigam perceber que o inglês não é minha língua materna.	1 2 3 4 5 6
28. Eu preciso estudar ou praticar fora de sala de aula para adquirir boa pronúncia em inglês.	1 2 3 4 5 6
29. Eu presto atenção à forma como as pessoas pronunciam palavras em inglês.	1 2 3 4 5 6

30. Eu presto atenção ao ritmo e à entonação quando outras pessoas falam em inglês.	1 2 3 4 5 6
31. Eu gosto de praticar inglês com falantes nativos em inglês.	1 2 3 4 5 6
32. É importante repetir e praticar bastante para adquirir boa pronúncia.	1 2 3 4 5 6
33. Eu gosto de conhecer pessoas de países de língua inglesa.	1 2 3 4 5 6
34. Programas de TV, música e filmes de países de língua inglesa me agradam.	1 2 3 4 5 6
35. Estudar inglês é importante, porque me possibilita entender melhor e apreciar o estilo de vida inglês/americano.	1 2 3 4 5 6
36. Eu gosto de inglês.	1 2 3 4 5 6
37. Para mim, a minha língua materna (português) é mais importante do que o inglês.	1 2 3 4 5 6
38. Eu prefiro música e filmes americanos/britânicos a música e filmes brasileiros.	1 2 3 4 5 6
39. Muitas vezes eu me imagino como alguém que sabe falar inglês bem.	1 2 3 4 5 6

Parte III

40. Por favor, avalie seu sotaque em uma escala de 9 (1= forte sotaque estrangeiro; 5= sotaque estrangeiro perceptível; 9= sotaque nativo). Circule somente um número:

1 2 3 4 5 6 7 8 9

Parte IV

41 Gênero:

☐ Masculino
☐ Feminino

42 Quantos anos você têm?

1. Menos de 18 anos ( )
2. 18--24 anos ( )
3. 25--34 anos ( )
4. 35--44 anos ( )
5. 45--54 anos ( )
6. 55--64 anos ( )
7. 65--74 anos ( )
8. 75 anos ou mais ( )

43. Com quantos anos você começou a aprender inglês?

1. Menos de 12 anos ( )
2. 12--17 anos ( )
3. 18--24 anos ( )
4. 25--34 anos ( )
5. 35--44 anos ( )
6. 45--54 anos ( )
7. 55--64 anos ( )
8. 65--74 anos ( )
9. 75 anos ou mais ( )

44. Há quanto tempo você está no Reino Unido?

1. Menos de 6 meses ( )
2. 7--11 meses ( )
3. 1--3 anos ( )
4. 4--6 anos ( )
5. 7--9 anos ( )
6. 10 anos ou mais ( )

45. Você já esteve em outro país de língua inglesa? Se sim, por quanto tempo?

1. Sim, por menos de 6 meses. ( )
2. Sim, de 7--11 meses. ( )
3. Sim, de 1--3 anos. ( )
4. Sim, de 4--6 anos. ( )
5. Sim, de 7--9 anos. ( )
6. Sim, por 10 anos ou mais. ( )
7. Não. ( )

46. Com qual frequência você fala português no Reino Unido? (1 = nunca; 5 =frequentemente)

1 2 3 4 5

47. Avalie os seguintes métodos de 1 a 3 de acordo com sua eficiência no aprendizado de pronúncia.

1. Exercícios de prática em sala de aula ( )
2. Estudo autônomo ( )
3. Viagem ao país onde a língua é falada ( )

48. Quão motivado você é para melhorar sua pronúncia? (1 = nem um pouco; 5 = bastante)

1 2 3 4 5

Parte V

49. Minha lições de pronúncia na escola são (satisfatórias/insatisfatórias).

*Por favor, especifique a razão.

_____

Muito obrigada pela sua ajuda!

Você gostaria de receber informação sobre os resultados deste estudo? Se sim, por favor, escreva seu e-mail abaixo e um resumo dos resultados será encaminhado quando o estudo terminar.

_____

APPENDIX 3

Questionnaire on Brazilian learners' beliefs about L2 English pronunciation

We would like to ask you to help us by answering the following questions concerning foreign language learning. This survey is conducted by the Institute of Education at University College London to better understand learners' beliefs about L2 English pronunciation. This is not a test so there are no "right" or "wrong" answers. We are interested in your personal opinion. Please give your answers sincerely, as only this will guarantee the success of the investigation. Thank you very much for your help.

Part I

In this part, we would like you to tell us how much you agree or disagree with the following statements by simply circling a number from 1 to 6. Please do not leave out any of the items.

Strongly Disagree	Disagree	Slightly Disagree	Slightly Agree	Agree	Strongly Agree
1	2	3	4	5	6

E.g., If you think that there is something true about this statement but it is somewhat exaggerated, you should circle 4 or 5.	
Chocolate is unhealthy.	1 2 3 4 5 6

1. It is easier for children than adults to use correct pronunciation.	1 2 3 4 5 6
2. Some people are born with a special ability which helps them learn and use correct foreign pronunciation.	1 2 3 4 5 6

3. Your proficiency in English pronunciation depends on factors you have little control over.	1 2 3 4 5 6
4. It is best to learn English pronunciation in an English speaking country.	1 2 3 4 5 6
5. Pronunciation instruction should be included in English classes.	1 2 3 4 5 6
6. I would take a pronunciation course if it were available to me.	1 2 3 4 5 6
7. Learning phonetic symbols (e.g., /æ/,/ʌ/,/ə/ etc.) in English classes can improve my pronunciation.	1 2 3 4 5 6
8. I believe that my teacher's production provides me with an excellent model of English pronunciation.	1 2 3 4 5 6
9. I feel at ease when I have to speak English.	1 2 3 4 5 6
10. I feel insecure about my pronunciation.	1 2 3 4 5 6
11. My pronunciation improves when I speak with non--native speakers.	1 2 3 4 5 6
12. I feel less anxious when I speak with non--native speakers of English.	1 2 3 4 5 6
13. Having a good pronunciation in English is important for my professional career.	1 2 3 4 5 6
14. A good pronunciation in English will permit me to become an influential member of my community.	1 2 3 4 5 6
15. A good pronunciation in English will allow me to interact more easily with native speakers of English.	1 2 3 4 5 6
16. A good pronunciation in English will allow me to interact more easily with speakers who do not speak my language.	1 2 3 4 5 6

Part II

These are new questions but please answer them the same way as you did before.

Strongly Disagree	Disagree	Slightly Disagree	Slightly Agree	Agree	Strongly Agree
1	2	3	4	5	6

17. I think I have foreign language aptitude (a special ability for learning foreign languages).	1 2 3 4 5 6
18. I believe I can eventually speak English very well.	1 2 3 4 5 6
19. I am happy with my present English pronunciation.	1 2 3 4 5 6
20. My English pronunciation is below the average.	1 2 3 4 5 6
21. Sometimes I can pass for a native speaker in brief interactions.	1 2 3 4 5 6
22. I try to imitate the pronunciation of native English speakers.	1 2 3 4 5 6
23. It is important for me to speak English with an excellent English pronunciation.	1 2 3 4 5 6
24. I do not like it when people recognize in my accent that I am not a native speaker of English.	1 2 3 4 5 6
25. I want to speak English with an accent that is not linked to a particular English speaking country.	1 2 3 4 5 6
26. I am happy with my pronunciation as long as people can understand me.	1 2 3 4 5 6
27. I don't mind that people can hear that English is not my first language.	1 2 3 4 5 6
28. I need to study or practice outside the classroom in order to acquire good English pronunciation.	1 2 3 4 5 6
29. I pay attention to how people pronounce words in English.	1 2 3 4 5 6
30. I pay attention to rhythm and intonation when other people speak English.	1 2 3 4 5 6
31. I enjoy practicing English with native English speakers.	1 2 3 4 5 6
32. It is important to repeat and practice a lot in order to acquire good pronunciation.	1 2 3 4 5 6
33. I like meeting people from English--speaking countries.	1 2 3 4 5 6

34. I am fond of TV programs, music, and movies from English--speaking countries.	1 2 3 4 5 6
35. Studying English is important because it will enable me to better understand and appreciate the English/American way of life.	1 2 3 4 5 6
36. I like English.	1 2 3 4 5 6
37. To me my mother tongue (Portuguese) is more important than English.	1 2 3 4 5 6
38. I prefer American/British movies and music to Brazilian movies and music.	1 2 3 4 5 6
39. I often imagine myself as someone who is able to speak English well.	1 2 3 4 5 6

Part III

40. Please rank your accent in English on a scale of 9 (1= heavy foreign accent; 5= noticeable foreign accent; 9=not accented at all). Circle only one number:

2 2 3 4 5 6 7 8 9

Part IV

Gender:

☐ Male
☐ Female

42 How old are you?

_____

43 At what age did you start learning English?

_____

44 How long have you been in the UK?

_____

45 Have you ever been in another English--speaking country? If so, for how long?

_____

46 How often do you speak Portuguese in the UK? (1=never; 5=very often)

1 2 3 4 5

47 Rank the following methods from 1 to 3 according to their efficiency in the learning of pronunciation.

   a.   practice exercises in class ( )
   b.   self--study ( )
   c.   stay--abroad ( )

48 How motivated are you to improve your pronunciation? (1=not at all; 5=very much) 1 2 3 4 5

Part V

49 My pronunciation lessons in school are (satisfactory/ unsatisfactory).
* Please specify the reason.

_____
_____

Thank you very much for your help!

Would you like to receive information about the findings of this study?

If so, please write your email below and a summary of the findings will be forwarded to when the study is finished.

_____

APPENDIX 4

Sources of questionnaire items

1. It is easier for children than adults to use correct pronunciation. *Horwitz (1985)*
2. Some people are born with a special ability which helps them learn and use correct foreign pronunciation. *Adapted from Horwitz (1985), Rieger (2009)*
3. Your proficiency in English pronunciation depends on factors you have little control over. *Simon and Taverniers (2011)*
4. It is best to learn English pronunciation in an English speaking country. *Adapted from Rieger (2009)*
5. Pronunciation instruction should be included in English classes. *Based on Derwing and Munro (2002)*
6. I would take a pronunciation course if it were available to me. *Based on Derwing and Munro (2002)*
7. Learning phonetic symbols (e.g., /æ/,/ʌ/,/ə/ etc.) in English classes can improve my pronunciation. *Based on Cenoz and Lecumberri (2005) and Sobkowiak (2002)*
8. I believe that my teacher's production provides me with an excellent model of English pronunciation. *Kang (2010)*
9. I feel at ease when I have to speak English. *Meerleer (2012), Rieger (2009)*
10. I feel insecure about my pronunciation. *Meerleer (2012), Rieger (2009)*
11. My pronunciation improves when I speak with non--native speakers. *Based on Takahashi (1989)*

12. I feel less anxious when I speak with non--native speakers of English.   *Based on Takahashi (1989)*
13. Having a good pronunciation in English is important for my professional career.   *Meerleer (2012), Simon and Taverniers (2011), Horwitz (1985), Rieger (2009)*
14. A good pronunciation in English will permit me to become an influential member of my community.   *Meerleer (2012)*
15. A good pronunciation in English will allow me to interact more easily with native speakers of English.   *Meerleer (2012)*
16. A good pronunciation in English will allow me to interact more easily with speakers who do not speak my language. *Meerleer (2012)*
17. I think I have foreign language aptitude (a special ability for learning foreign languages).   *Horwitz (1985)*
18. I believe I can eventually speak English very well.   *Kaypak and Ortaçtepe (2014), Elliot (1995), Horwitz (1985), Yang (1999)*
19. I am happy with my present English pronunciation.   *Meerleer (2012), Sifakis and Sougari (2005)*
20. My English pronunciation is below the average.   *Adapted from Kaypak and Ortaçtepe (2014)*
21. Sometimes I can pass for a native speaker in brief interactions.   *Based on Piller (2002)*
22. I try to imitate the pronunciation of native English speakers. Nowacka (2012), Pullen (2012)
23. It is important for me to speak English with an excellent English pronunciation.   *Horwitz (1985), Yang (1999), Nowacka (2012), Moyer (1999), Smit (2002), Sobkowiak (2002)*
24. I do not like it when people recognize in my accent that I am not a native speaker of English. *Meerleer (2012), Smit (2002)*

25. I want to speak English with an accent that is not linked to a particular English speaking country.   *Meerleer (2012), Kaypak and Ortaçtepe (2014)*
26. I am happy with my pronunciation as long as people can understand me.   *Meerleer (2012), Elliot (1995)*
27. I don't mind that people can hear that English is not my first language.   *Meerleer (2012), Cenoz and Lecumberri (2005), Kaypak and Ortaçtepe (2014)*
28. I need to study or practice outside the classroom in order to acquire good English pronunciation.   *Adapted from Kaypak and Ortaçtepe (2014)*
29. I pay attention to how people pronounce words in English.   *Derwing and Rossiter (2002), Yang (1999)*
30. I pay attention to rhythm and intonation when other people speak English.   *Derwing and Rossiter (2002)*
31. I enjoy practicing English with native English speakers.   *Adapted from Rieger (2009), Cenoz and Lecumberri (2005)*
32. It is important to repeat and practice a lot in order to acquire good pronunciation.   *Adapted from Horwitz (1985)*
33. I like meeting people from English--speaking countries.   *Based on El--Dash & Busnardo (2001), Pullen, 2012, Smit (2002)*
34. I am fond of TV programs, music, and movies from English--speaking countries.   *Based on El--Dash & Busnardo (2001, Pullen (2012), Smit (2002)*
35. Studying English is important because it will enable me to better understand and appreciate the English/American way of life. *Meerleer (2012)*
36. I like English.   *Ryan (2009), Kaypak and Ortaçtepe (2014)*

37. To me my mother tongue (Portuguese) is more important than English.
Based on El--Dash & Busnardo (2001), Pullen (2012), Smit (2002)
38. I prefer American/British movies and music to Brazilian movies and music.
Based on El--Dash & Busnardo (2001), Pullen (2012), Smit (2002)
39. I often imagine myself as someone who is able to speak English well.
Ryan (2009)

APPENDIX 5

Subject Sheet

You will have a series of three tasks, and you should NOT "PAUSE" between each task. Please record according to the order of tasks presented. Use the "PAUSE" button at the end of the recording, but DO NOT use rewind or fast forward.

Please read the following words at a natural pace.

Task 1: word items

1. Insight
2. envelope
3. bilingualism
4. apple
5. milk
6. pool
7. worked
8. played
9. feminism
10. special
11. small
12. Internet
13. beat

Task 2: sentence items

1. I think the boat sank.
2. The road sign is green.
3. The cat went to the park.
4. Kate moves the pot and pans.
5. The girl listens to rap music.
6. I didn't talk to Peter, I talked to Mary.
7. They never greet each other.
8. I read easy books.
9. The judge looked like he was in a bad mood.
10. Cash the check, said Pete.

Task 3: free-response items

Please respond to ONE of the following items. Your response need be only 5--10 sentences.

a. Describe your daily routine: what you normally do, when, with whom, for how long, what's interesting about it etc.
b. Describe an experience you had which was meaningful in your life: Who was involved? How old were you? How did this influence you?
c. Describe a person in your life who means a lot to you: How do you know this person? Why is he/she significant in your life?

PAUSE
Thank you for participating!!

APPENDIX 6

Rater Sheet

Please rate the speech samples on a scale of 9 (1= heavy foreign accent; 5= noticeable foreign accent; 9= not accented at all).

Speech Samples	1	2	3	4	5	6	7	8	9
1									
2									
3									
4									
5									
6									
7									
8									
9									
10									
11									
12									
13									
14									
15									
16									
17									

18									
19									
20									
21									
22									
23									
24									
25									
26									
27									
28									
29									
30									

APPENDIX 7

Non-significant correlations: questionnaire items

It is easier for children than adults to use correct pronunciation.   r = .11, p = .54, p > .05
3. Your proficiency in English pronunciation depends on factors you have little control over.   r = -- .36, p = .18, p > .05
5. Pronunciation instruction should be included in English classes.   r = -- .15, p = 42, p > .05
7. Learning phonetic symbols (e.g., /æ/,/ʌ/,/ə/ etc.) in English classes can improve my pronunciation.   r = .00, p = .96, p > .05
12. I feel less anxious when I speak with non--native speakers of English.   r = -- .29, p = .12, p > .05
13. Having a good pronunciation in English is important for my professional career.   r = -- .03, p = .84, p > .05
14. A good pronunciation in English will permit me to become an influential member of my community.   r = .00, p = .96, p > .05
15. A good pronunciation in English will allow me to interact more easily with native speakers of English.   r = -- .13, p = .47, p > .05
16. A good pronunciation in English will allow me to interact more easily with speakers who do not speak my language.   r = -- .23, p = .51, p > .05

17. I think I have foreign language aptitude (a special ability for learning foreign languages). r = .21, p = .56, p > .05
18. I believe I can eventually speak English very well. r = .20, p = .29, p > .05
21. Sometimes I can pass for a native speaker in brief interactions. r = .08, p = .65, p > 05
29. I pay attention to how people pronounce words in English. r = .10, p = .59, p > .05
30. I pay attention to rhythm and intonation when other people speak English. r = .11, p = .55, p > .05
31. I enjoy practicing English with native English speakers. r = .10, p = .57, p > .05
32. It is important to repeat and practice a lot in order to acquire good pronunciation. r = -- .04, p = .81, p > .05
34. I am fond of TV programs, music, and movies from English--speaking countries. r = .06, p = .72, p > .05
35. Studying English is important because it will enable me to better understand and appreciate the Englrish/American way of life. r = .03, p = .85, p > .05
36. I like English. r = .29, p = .12, p > .05
37. To me my mother tongue (Portuguese) is more important than English. r = -- .06, p = .73, p > .05
38. I prefer American/British movies and music to Brazilian movies and music. r = -- .24, p = .20, p > .05
39. I often imagine myself as someone who is able to speak English well. r = .17, p = .40, p > .05

APPENDIX 8

Master's Dissertation Awards, British Council

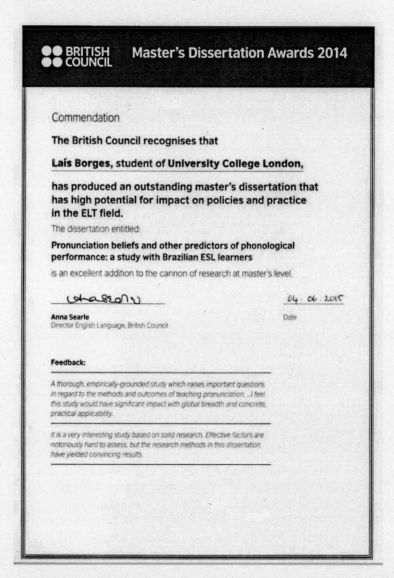